"I've never seen a single book that covers the waterfront of ethical issues in a biblically faithful way at a level available to high school readers. That is, until now. *Love Your Neighbor* is clear, concise, broad, biblical, and readable."

> — J. P. MORELAND, Distinguished Professor of Philosophy,
> Talbot School of Theology, Biola University

"Those looking for simplistic answers will not find them here; those willing to grapple with both the Bible and real life will welcome this opportunity to think carefully about the choices that confront us every single day."

> —ERWIN LUTZER, Senior Pastor, The Moody Church, Chicago

"Though they tackle head-on the key philosophical questions, Geisler and Snuffer write in a style that will be easily understood and greatly appreciated by youth and adults alike."

> —JOSH D. McDOWELL, author and speaker

"Geisler and Snuffer show how the triune God and 'the greatest commandment' help us navigate through the array of difficult questions that challenge us today."

> —RAVI ZACHARIAS, author and speaker

"*Love Your Neighbor* addresses the moral issues of our day from a distinctly biblical position. How encouraging to see the basic issues of lying, cheating, and stealing addressed along with the more obvious things people think about."

> — PAIGE PATTERSON, President, Southwestern Baptist
> Theological Seminary

"*Love Your Neighbor* avoids telling us what to believe or how to behave in any given situation, but presents clear guidelines to help us determine where the high ground can be found."

> — JOHN F. ANKERBERG, President, Ankerberg Theological
> Research Institute

To Mindy,

Neil Gaiman

LOVE YOUR NEIGHBOR

Thinking Wisely about Right and Wrong

NORMAN L. GEISLER
AND RYAN P. SNUFFER

CROSSWAY BOOKS
WHEATON, ILLINOIS

Love Your Neighbor: Thinking Wisely about Right and Wrong

Copyright © 2007 by Norman L. Geisler and Ryan P. Snuffer

Published by Crossway Books
a publishing ministry of Good News Publishers
1300 Crescent Street
Wheaton, Illinois 60187

Cover design: Jon McGrath

Cover photo: Getty Images

Scripture quotations are from *The Holy Bible, English Standard Version*® (ESV®), copyright © 2001 by Crossway Bibles, a publishing ministry of Good News Publishers. Used by permission. All rights reserved.

All emphasis in Scripture quotations has been added by the authors.

Library of Congress Cataloging-in-Publication Data
Geisler, Norman L.
  Love your neighbor : thinking wisely about right and wrong /
Norman L. Geisler and Ryan P. Snuffer.
    p. cm.
  Includes bibliographical references and index.
  ISBN 13: 978-1-58134-945-0 (tpb)
  ISBN 13: 978-1-58134-945-9
  1. Christian ethics—Textbooks. 2. Young adults—Conduct of life—
Textbooks. I. Snuffer, Ryan P., 1974–   . II. Title.
BJ1261.G455   2007
241—dc22   2007010483

BP   17   16   15   14   13   12   11   10   09   08   07
15   14   13   12   11   10   9   8   7   6   5   4   3   2   1

CONTENTS

ILLUSTRATIONS

Part One

INTRODUCTION TO CHRISTIAN ETHICS

Chapter 1

THE NATURE
OF GOD

"GOD" IS A GENERAL TERM that takes on many meanings in many different cultural contexts. Various pantheistic religions, such as Hinduism, Buddhism, and New Age cults, define "god" as an impersonal force that is in some way equated to an eternal universe. The idea of a pantheistic God is in direct conflict with the idea of a theistic God. The monotheistic religions of the world (Christianity, Judaism, Islam) view God as personal and separate from His creation. The ethical approach of this text is based on a monotheistic or theistic concept of God—a God who is absolute in His nature, resulting in absolute moral ideas. It is not the purpose of this text to prove that theism is true or that Christianity is superior to the other theistic religions. One would need to study theology or apologetics to establish these ideas. From this point it will be assumed that theism, and in particular, biblical Christianity, is true.[1]

Various terms related to God will be used throughout this text. It is important to know the attributes of God if one is to understand the ethical approach of the biblical Christian. The theistic God's attributes can be divided into two categories—those that relate to His infinite nature and those that relate to

---

[1]There are many good apologetics resources for those interested in this study. A companion to this text dealing more specifically with apologetics is Ryan P. Snuffer, *Truth in Focus* (Longwood, Fla.: Xulon, 2005). See also Norman L. Geisler and Frank Turek, *I Don't Have Enough Faith to Be an Atheist* (Wheaton, Ill.: Crossway, 2004).

His moral nature. God's infinite attributes are aspects of His nature or essence. His moral attributes relate to His morality. These attributes collectively define who the theistic God is. There is likely much more to His nature than what has been revealed to us. This is just an introduction to what we know through reason and the sacred writings of the Bible.

INFINITE

Eternality. Isaiah 57:15 teaches that God dwells in a higher realm known as eternity. "For thus says the One who is high and lifted up, who inhabits eternity, whose name *is* Holy: 'I dwell in the high and holy place.'" The eternal realm is beyond time and space. Time had a beginning. Eternity gave birth to time. Eternity is the infinite abode of God. Humans can only speculate about this aspect of reality. Some see eternity as a higher dimension beyond time. God is not limited in His nature and is therefore not limited to time. He can view all of history simultaneously.

Transcendence. This term simply means that God is beyond this universe. This is in contrast to the pantheistic view that God *is* the universe. God created the universe apart from Himself; He is not subject to its physical laws but in control of them.

Immanence. God is not only beyond this universe, He is also present within it.

Omnipotence. God is all-powerful. He is sovereign over His creation and has the power to act within it and control what happens.

Omniscience. God is all-knowing. There is nothing that happens that surprises God. Since He sees all of history simultaneously, He knows all things. He not only knows everything that has happened or will happen, but He is aware of every possible event. He knows every possible outcome of every possible choice or event.

Omnipresence. God is everywhere present in the universe.

Immutability. God cannot change. He cannot change anything about His nature. For example, He cannot cease to be eternal; He cannot cease to exist.

MORAL

Love. The Bible often repeats the idea that God is love or that God loves. He loves His creation. In particular, He loves human beings.

Holiness. God is morally perfect. He is wholly incapable of sinning in thought or action. Evil is a privation of something good. God is morally complete and therefore perfectly holy.

Truth. God cannot lie. He always acts truthfully, speaks honestly, and thinks and acts consistently with Himself.

Mercy. God does not always give us what we deserve. The writers of the Bible often prayed for mercy in spite of their sin. Mercy is related to forgiveness.

Grace. God gives to people positive blessings that they do not necessarily deserve.

Justice. God will always do what is right. He will reward goodness and judge sin.

Of the above moral attributes, love, truth, justice, and holiness can be thought of as something God is. Mercy and grace are actions that God does in accordance with who He is. It could be said that the last four attributes are in some way logically based on love and holiness. For example, God extends mercy and grace because of His love and compassion. These attributes coexist harmoniously without conflict.

LIMITATIONS OF GOD

Even though God is infinite, He cannot do everything. He can do only what is possible, and some things are not possible.

Some people are offended with the idea that God cannot do everything. Perhaps they have sung a few too many verses of

the children's song "God can do anything, anything, anything
. . . but sin." Consider the fact that God cannot make a square
circle. Before you say, "He could if He wanted to," bear in mind
that this is a logical impossibility.

The fact that God is infinite in His nature does not imply
that He can do anything. Here is a partial list of things that God
cannot do:

1. God cannot sin (such as break an unconditional promise).
   To say that God could sin would limit or conflict with
   His holiness. God is complete in His holiness. The ability to sin would mean that His holiness is not complete.
   Therefore God cannot sin, or even be tempted with sin
   (James 1:13).
2. God cannot change His essence or act against His nature
   (such as cease to exist). God's nature is perfect. Therefore
   He has no need to change. Even the possibility of change
   would indicate a less than infinite nature. Malachi 3:6
   states that God does not change.
3. God cannot do that which is logically impossible. To
   say that God could make a square circle or a rock so big
   that He could not pick it up is logically impossible. God
   cannot do that which is logically impossible. (Sometimes
   human "logic" is not correct; therefore, God could do
   that which would *seem* to oppose logic, but in actuality,
   God is being logical. It is the human who is mistaken.)

These limitations should not make us think less of God.
They should bring comfort and security in knowing that He can
be trusted. Though humans cannot grasp the mind of God, He
can be understood rationally to the extent that He has revealed
Himself to humanity.

CONCLUSION

The theistic God is eternal, powerful, infinite, holy, and loving. He exists independently from His creation. His essence

or nature cannot be changed; it is absolute. If there is a moral code of ethics that stems from God's nature, it would also be absolute. God is limited only by those things that are logically impossible or those things that would be in conflict with His nature, such as sinning or ceasing to exist.

DISCUSSION/APPLICATION:

1. Do the attributes of God listed in this chapter bring feelings of inspiration or of fear?
2. Is it a new concept for you to consider God as having limitations?
3. Circle the following attributes or characteristics that are related to God's infinite nature, not His activity:

Eternality	Justice	Love
Holiness	Mercy	Immanence
Omniscience	Transcendence	Truth
Immutability	Omnipotence	Grace

Chapter 2

THE NATURE OF
MORALITY

THERE ARE MANY TOUGH questions related to morality
that people are asking today.

- Is there such a thing as right or wrong?
- Can it be said that certain things are always right or always
  wrong?
- Isn't it harder to be morally pure in this day and age than
  it was a hundred years ago?
- Is it not true that much of what humans accept as right or
  wrong is related to a person's particular culture?

The answers to these questions are related to the nature of
God and truth. God's nature is absolute in the sense that it does
not change. Those aspects of God which are moral in nature
(love, truth, holiness, mercy, grace, and justice) are therefore
absolute. For example, love is absolutely right. Holiness is
absolutely right. It is morally proper to show grace and mercy.
Justice is equal to righteousness—that which is right.

We know these things about God based on two types of revelation. First, the Bible declares these things to be true. Second,
nature itself teaches these things to be true. The human conscience bears witness to the truth that some things are right and
some things are wrong. Philosophers refer to this innate sense
of right and wrong as the moral law. This is one of the main

reasons C. S. Lewis converted from atheism to Christianity. Notice what he writes: "Human beings, all over the earth, have this curious idea that they ought to behave in a certain way, and cannot really get rid of it."[1] This curious idea is related to a standard outside of themselves. The only way something can be measured is by a standard. A girl can know how tall she is only by comparing herself to a standard, such as a tape measure or another person whose height has been measured.

How is it that people instinctively know that something is either right or wrong? In order for humans to know the difference between right and wrong, there must be an objective standard beyond or independent of the human race. There cannot be a law without a lawgiver. Evidence suggests that there is a universal moral law; therefore, there must be a moral lawgiver, namely, God.

The evidence for this law is so strong that some scientists have suggested that there might be a type of gene that guides human instinct about behavior.[2] This instinct is different than the type of instinct that guides a bird south for the winter and back to its home the following summer. An animal's instinct consistently guides its behavior. However, this human idea of the moral law is different in that, although humans know what is right and wrong, they don't always live consistently with what they know they should do.

Murder is absolutely wrong for several reasons related to the nature of God. For instance, it is unloving, unmerciful, and unjust to take away the life of an innocent person. Because it is absolutely right to love and be just, it is absolutely wrong to murder. It is also unloving to steal or to commit adultery with someone else's spouse. Of course, since God is sovereign over each life that He created, He has the right to take it (Job 1:21). But since we did not create it, we have no right to take it.

God did not arbitrarily make up a list of rules for all morally

---

[1]C. S. Lewis, *Mere Christianity* (San Francisco: HarperCollins, 2001), 8. First published in 1952.
[2]Dean Hamer, "Are We Born with a God Gene?" *Charlotte Observer*, October 4, 2004, 17A.

aware beings to keep. What can be considered absolutely right or wrong is that which flows from His absolute nature. If there is a rule that does not necessarily flow from God's nature, then it cannot be thought of as absolute. The differences between an absolute moral idea and a rule that can change will be illustrated in more detail in chapter 3 on "The Old Testament Law."

The system of ethics that will be discussed in this text is based on a view of truth and God that is absolute. The various issues that will be discussed will be viewed in light of Scripture and culture. Some of these issues will be easy to deal with because the issues are closely connected to one of God's moral attributes and are dealt with in the Bible. Other issues will not be as clear, but will require an examination of biblical principles and common sense. Any position that conflicts with God's nature can be easily dismissed as incorrect or wrong.

SUMMARY

Some moral positions can be considered absolutely right or wrong. What these positions are can be known by whether they are clearly consistent with or clearly in conflict with God's nature. Some things may be based on cultural preferences or needs. The question, Isn't it harder to be morally pure in this day and age than it was a hundred years ago? is the wrong question. No one in any culture has ever lived a completely holy life. A better question is, What is God's will for my life morally? A study of ethics in light of biblical principles will shed light on this question. For the Christian, recognizing what is right and wrong and then acknowledging an inability to be perfect is the first step to finding God's will.

DISCUSSION/APPLICATION:

1. Why do so many people today cringe at the idea of absolute moral truth? How do the media contribute to people's tendency to reject absolute moral truth?
2. Some would object to the idea of a moral law by pointing

out that many people have different opinions about particular issues such as homosexuality or gambling. Consider, however, the issues of murder, rape, and theft. Though the specific definition of murder may vary slightly from one culture to another, every culture considers murder to be wrong. This is likewise true with rape and theft. People instinctively know that honesty is better than deceit. By what standard can a person say that some particular action is truly better than some other particular action, if there is no moral law?

3. What do you consider some of the most important moral truths in relation to your personal life? What about in your family? What about in society?

4. Speculate about what a society that did not have churches or other institutions attempting to instruct society about morality might be like.

Chapter 3

THE OLD
TESTAMENT LAW

MOST PEOPLE WHO grew up in the 1950s or earlier can recall seeing the Ten Commandments proudly displayed in courtrooms, school principals' offices, and other public venues. The 1960s brought both positive and negative social changes in our society. The push for racial equality was an important step in the right direction during that time. However, many evangelicals today blame the generation of the 1960s for taking God out of society by, in part, removing the Ten Commandments from all public, government supported institutions. The fires of controversy were reignited when Alabama Supreme Court Chief Justice Roy Moore refused to remove from the courthouse a 5,280-pound granite rock on which the Ten Commandments were proudly displayed. Though the majority of Americans are comfortable with public displays of religion as long as they are not forced on people, many influential Americans believe that the separation of church and state means there should be no public displays of religion in courtrooms, public schools, or other public buildings.

The Ten Commandments are found in Exodus 20 of the Old Testament. They deal with human relations to God and human relations to other humans. The other world religions support the majority of these commands. C. S. Lewis makes a strong case that the majority of these commands have been universally assumed in the major cultures throughout history.[1] He is correct in asserting that most people throughout history have embraced a code of ethics very similar to the Ten Commandments; however, not all individuals are in agreement with these laws.

Some detractors point out that in order to establish an Old Testament system of Law, one would have to establish a sort of theocracy (rule by God). Detractors also point out that there were about twenty different sins that people were put to death for in the Old Testament. These sins included murder, witchcraft, homosexuality, blasphemy, and rebelliousness. There were other laws about not eating pork, sacrificing animals, not touching dead bodies, and not working on Saturday that would be difficult to sell in today's world. Why should Christians be able to pick and choose which aspects of the Law to enforce and which ones to ignore?

The answer is that they should not. The Old Testament Law was established for a particular time and people in history. Christian doctrine teaches that Jesus Christ fulfilled the Mosaic Law. Early Christian leaders established a new idea sometimes referred to as Christian liberty.[2] Christians should not arbitrarily choose the parts of the Bible that best suit their own ethical ideas. Christians do not need to do this because Jesus showed us a better way, which will be discussed in the next chapter.

One of the reasons for the disharmony in opinions about the Law among believers is ignorance. The "Old Testament Law" is actually a complex set of rules and rituals for the Jewish people before the coming of their Messiah, Jesus. Many of these rules and rituals were based on the need for personal cleanliness. Others were symbolic of God Himself. For example, the purposes of the temple and its associated rituals were fulfilled by the death of Christ on the cross. They were meant as a visual,

---

[1]C. S. Lewis, *Mere Christianity* (San Francisco: HarperCollins, 2001), 8. First published in 1952.
[2]Appendix A addresses the idea of Christian liberty.

practical tutor to help the people understand their need for forgiveness and mercy from God. Since Christ fulfilled the Law, what use is there for us today for these ancient writings?

There were different aspects to the Old Testament Law. Though most of the 613 commands from the Old Testament were temporal, the basis for many of these commands is God's absolute nature. For example, a man who commits murder should be put to death. Though God is not necessarily telling us to put all murderers to death today, He is still telling us that murder is wrong. It is absolutely wrong to take away the life of an "innocent" human being made in the image of God. It is absolutely wrong for a man to rape a woman or molest a child. Table 3.1 will help summarize the various aspects of the Law.

Table 3.1
Aspects of the Mosaic Law

	Civil	Ceremonial	Moral
Types of laws	Stoning homosexuals; thieves repaying seven times the amount they stole	Temple sacrifices; cleansing laws	Do not bear false witness; do not covet; do not murder; do not commit adultery
Applicability	Practical application of moral law; the application is not absolute but changes from OT to NT	Fulfilled by Christ	Absolute; based on God's unchanging nature

As the table depicts, only one of these categories of Old Testament Law is absolute. Furthermore, the ideas under "Moral" law are not unique to the Old Testament. These ideas are found abundantly in the writings of the other religions of the world, and in the New Testament. They seem to be common sense to most people. People often feel guilty when they break these commands, even if they have never read the Bible.

The Ten Commandments come close to encapsulating

this idea of God's moral law. All except the fourth command, to remember the Sabbath, are repeated by Christ in the New Testament. The Jewish Sabbath was designated for a particular time in history, but the principle of the Sabbath remains. There are times in our lives in which work and play should be set aside for a time of worship. Whether a government like the United States should endorse these ideas or should mandate its citizens to follow these ideas is a subject we'll save for another chapter.

One should be careful not to make the mistake of thinking that there were three kinds of laws in the Old Testament and that one is binding and the other two are not. There was only one Old Testament Law. Nowhere in either Testament is there a clear distinction made among the three aspects of the Law. These are simply observations made by people who study the Bible. The entire system of law was abolished when Christ fulfilled the Law by His life, death, and resurrection. But part of the system is based on God's unchanging moral nature and therefore transcends any system, whether ethical, religious, or political. This same basic moral law, which reflects the unchanging nature of God, is written on the hearts of all persons (Rom. 2:12–15) and was called by the American Declaration of Independence "Nature's Laws" which came from "Nature's God."

DISCUSSION/APPLICATION:

1. Find an example in one of the books of Moses of each aspect of the Law:
   a. Civil:
   b. Ceremonial:
   c. Moral:
2. Paul wrote in Romans 2:14–15 that God has written His law on people's hearts and that their conscience bears witness to it. List and describe three examples that demonstrate

that people universally have the moral law written on their hearts. In other words, list three things that are taboo in almost every culture of the world.

1.

2.

3.

3. List five ways in which removing the Ten Commandments from the public arena in America may have affected morality in America.

1.

2.

3.

4.

5.

Chapter 4

THE HEART OF
THE LAW

A CRITICAL PHARISEE ASKED Jesus,

> "Teacher, which is the great commandment in the Law?" And
> he said to him, "You shall love the Lord your God with all your
> heart and with all your soul and with all your mind. This is the
> great and first commandment. And a second is like it: You shall
> love your neighbor as yourself. On these two commandments
> depend all the Law and the Prophets" (Matt. 22:36-40).

Jesus was trying to make an important point to a group of
legalistic Jews who felt secure in their spirituality because of the
external standards to which they had managed to conform. It
is not stricter standards that the Bible equates with holiness.
It is an honest heart that both loves and fears God. Strict, arbi-
trary standards are associated with legalism, a "seared" conscience (1 Tim. 4:1–5), and being spiritually weak (Romans 14;
1 Corinthians 10). However, no one can accuse Jesus of having
"loose" standards. He actually took important teaching from
the Law and elevated the standard by focusing on the internal
motive. According to Jesus, hatred is akin to murder and lust is
a form of adultery (Matthew 5:21-22, 27–28). Jesus consistently
emphasized one's motivation for any particular action over the
action itself.

When one looks at the Ten Commandments in light of

Jesus' two great commands, it becomes clear what the heart of the Law is: love. A person who really loves God will worship Him, not blaspheme His name, and not worship idols in His place. A person who truly loves his neighbor will not murder him, steal from him, commit adultery with his wife, or covet his possessions. A child or adult who loves her parents will honor them.

When striving to "keep the Law" by keeping a lengthy list of regulations, one learns quickly that it is impossible to do so. Some respond in frustration by moving toward anarchy or lawlessness. Others see their failures and understand better why Christ had to die on the cross for their sins.

Because of the law, whether in the written form of the Ten Commandments or the unwritten law stamped on the heart of every human being, everyone experiences guilt. Rather than trying to overcome guilt by keeping a longer, stricter list of "holy" standards, we should admit our guilt before God, ask Him to forgive us based on the finished work of Christ on the cross, and begin to pursue a love relationship with God.

Knowing what is right and wrong is important so that we can see where we fall short. However, the way to holiness is not found in doing good. The way to holiness is through a relationship with God. As we get closer to Him, we will not only be doing more good but we will *want* to do good. Love is the proper motivation for all moral choices.

Love is a moral absolute that is inseparably connected to God. Both God and humans should be thought of as an end, not as a means to an end. In other words, being a Christian as a means to becoming happy, wealthy, or secure has nothing to do with loving God. Using God to stay out of hell is a means to an end; loving God focuses on God as the object of desire and admiration. Loving God requires a focus on and knowledge of the object of our love, which is God Himself. Loving people is not the same as using people for your personal gain. One who truly loves seeks the happiness and pleasure of the object of his or her love.

The greatest example of sacrificial love is found in the idea of sacrifice. God was willing to sacrifice His own Son because of His love for human beings. A human father would do this for his own child. We are to love God and other humans with this same passionate desire. It is a fierce loyalty that readily prefers the happiness of the object rather than oneself. This kind of love can be possible only if one has a relationship with the Ultimate Lover. First John 4:19 states, "We love because he first loved us."

DISCUSSION/APPLICATION:

1. Read 1 Corinthians 13. Contrast love as defined in this chapter with the cheap imitation for love that is so prevalent in society today. Make two lists, one from 1 Corinthians 13 and the other from the way the world views love.

2. Would you rather have a marriage to someone who loves you or to someone who is just there to use you? This being the case, how do you think God regards the kind of love you have for Him? How could you grow in your love for God?

Chapter 5

RELATIVISTIC ETHICAL SYSTEMS

THE VARIOUS VIEWS ON how to approach ethics can be summarized in six categories. Two are based on a relativistic view of truth. A relativistic system views truth as being able to change in relation to one's perspective, such as culture, race, sex, or time in history. Four ethical approaches are based on an absolutist view of truth. Within an absolute system, truth is viewed as something that does not change.[1] This chapter will describe two relativistic approaches and then offer a few criticisms of each approach.

These two approaches to ethics allow human judgment to take precedence over any sort of divine absolute. These approaches are subjective in nature. People who embrace these approaches are usually atheistic and/or humanistic in their worldview. These views are summarized in Table 5.1.

Table 5.1
Relativistic Ethical Approaches

Antinomianism	Generalism
There are no moral laws.	There are some general laws, but no absolute ones.

---

[1]For lessons on truth beyond what you will find in this text see Ryan P. Snuffer, *Truth in Focus* (Longwood, Fla.: Xulon, 2005). For a more detailed overview of truth see Norman L. Geisler, *Baker Encyclopedia of Christian Apologetics* (Grand Rapids, Mich.: Baker, 1998).

ANTINOMIANISM

Antinomianism ("against law") does not wrestle with whether something is right or wrong; it does not allow for or acknowledge any moral laws. A particular ethic, such as lying, is neither right nor wrong. "Antinomianism is a radical form of ethical relativism. It denies not only that there are any valid ethical absolutes, but also that there are any binding moral laws whatsoever."[2]

In order to state that there are no absolutes, however, one must make an absolute claim. It is like saying there are absolutely no absolutes. In this sense, antinomianism is self-defeating. It is also illogical in the sense that it allows for two opposing views to both be correct. How can two contradictory ideas both be correct at the same time and in the same sense? (More about this in chapter 9.)

Besides being illogical, antinomianism is not practical. No society can function well without some restrictions related to moral behavior. A society without ethical laws would be in a state of moral anarchy. Anarchy leads to chaos. Someone or some group would try to restore order. Out of the chaos would likely arise a tyrannical system that would result in very little freedom at all. This system would then try to impose its own morality.

From a biblical perspective, antinomianism seems to be motivated by a heart of rebellion. The Bible associates lawlessness with the "spirit of the antichrist" (see 1 John 4:3 and 2 Thess. 2:3). It is certainly not a viable ethical option for Christians.

GENERALISM

Generalism seems to be one of the most common ethical approaches today. According to this view, general laws are

---

[2]Norman L. Geisler, *Christian Ethics: Options and Issues* (Grand Rapids, Mich.: Baker, 1989), 41.

established for the purpose of practicality. There are binding moral principles people can follow to make for a better society. Yet these principles are not absolute. They can change as the people of a given culture change. Laws that will benefit the greatest number of people are preferred. The results of the law determine its value; there is no intrinsic value in the law itself. In other words, laws are not made because something is absolutely right or wrong, but because something seems to work. This approach is utilitarian: right is defined as that which brings the greatest good to the greatest number of people over time.

There are several reasons to reject generalism as an ethical system. Without absolutes, generalism tends to move in the direction of antinomianism. "Unless there are some objective moral prescriptions of substantive content which are binding on all persons at all times, then at any given time it is possible that any action could be justified."[3] Within this system, one might ask, on what basis should I do anything? If for the good of the majority, then on what basis do we determine what is good for the majority? And why is it not also good for the minority?

DISCUSSION/APPLICATION:

1. Can you imagine what it would be like to shop at a retail store in which employees had no rules by which to abide? They could show up and leave whenever they wanted. They could dress however they wanted. They could talk to you anyway they wanted. They could refuse to help you or check you out. Besides being a business that would not stay open very long, what problems would you run into as a shopper? How does having ethical standards in the workplace make for a better society? Though antinomians do not advocate a society without any civil laws, they do advocate a society that has no laws based on moral absolutes. What sort of chaos might occur in a society without objective moral laws?

---

[3]Ibid., 79.

2. It seems that generalism would work better in a society than antinomianism; however, if there is no objective basis for moral laws, what might eventually happen in a society that is based on generalism?
3. In what ways does Western culture resemble the ethical approach of generalism?

RECOMMENDED READING

Geisler, Norman L. *Christian Ethics: Options and Issues.* Grand Rapids, Mich.: Baker, 1989.

Chapter 6

ABSOLUTIST ETHICAL SYSTEMS (PART 1)

THE UNIFYING FACTOR OF the following ethical systems is that they are based on at least one absolute. In theory, these are objective standards. Actions and ideas are defined as either right or wrong depending on how they compare to the objective standard. The Judeo-Christian worldview is based on what is considered divine revelation. Evangelical Christians base their ethic on the Bible, which they view as a revelation of God Himself. There is much agreement within the Bible-believing community about many of the issues in this text. The disagreement often revolves around how to apply these ethical standards in a society. The four ethical approaches depicted in Table 6.1 summarize the absolutist positions (the first two of which we will examine in this chapter). Most evangelicals fall within one of the latter three categories.

Table 6.1
Absolutist Ethical Approaches

Situationism	Unqualified Absolutism	Conflicting Absolutism	Graded Absolutism
There is only one absolute: love.	There are many absolutes that never conflict with each other.	There are many absolutes that sometimes conflict with each other, and it is always wrong to disobey any of them.	There are many absolutes that sometimes conflict with each other, and it is always right to follow the higher law.

SITUATIONISM

"Contrary to what the word situationism might seem to imply, it is not a completely normless ethic. According to one of its most vigorous proponents, Joseph Fletcher, author of *Situation Ethics,* situationism is located between the extremes of legalism and antinomianism. The antinomians have no laws, the legalists have laws for everything, and Fletcher's situationism has only one law."[1] Others have written about this ethical approach, but Fletcher's position remains the most popular.

Situationists might quote Jesus, but He stated that all of the Law and the Prophets hang on two commands—to love God and to love one's neighbor—not just one. Situationists see people as having real value. Things have value only because people value them. Because people have value, they should be treated lovingly. Situationists also seek for what is practical for love's sake.

Situationism is a form of absolutism in the sense that it does establish love as the one absolute; it is relativism in the sense that every ethical idea is relative to love, and love turns out to be an empty concept. Within every ethical dilemma, one should ask, what is the loving thing to do? Though situationism is based on the one absolute of love, it is subjective because love is not defined in absolute terms. What one person may consider loving, another may reject as cruel. Though situationism may seem to be a good option, it often lacks the stability and practicality of the other absolutist positions. Situationists often attempt to do what is most loving for the greatest number of people. Fletcher would adopt an "end justifies the means" mentality.[2]

UNQUALIFIED ABSOLUTISM

Unqualified absolutism says there are many absolutes and that these absolutes never come into conflict with each other. This

---

[1]Norman L. Geisler, *Christian Ethics: Options and Issues* (Grand Rapids, Mich.: Baker, 1989), 43.
[2]Ibid., 60.

approach strives for consistency and takes issue with the view that God would allow people to be in situations in which they would have to break an absolute moral norm. This system is one of the most widely held approaches within Christianity. Notable philosophers and theologians who have promoted this view include Augustine, Immanuel Kant, and Charles Hodge.

If there seems to be a moral conflict, the unqualified absolutist would say that it is not a real conflict but only an apparent one. Lying to prevent a rape or murder would not be acceptable to unqualified absolutists. They insist that God will only reward good behavior, and that since lying is a sin, one must tell the truth and leave the results up to God.

Kant taught that an action is intrinsically either good or evil. It cannot be allowed that a lie can be good in one situation and bad in another. The evangelical theologian John Murray taught that God's law is absolutely binding. The will of God is a sovereign reflection of His unchanging character. Since God is truth and cannot ever lie (Heb. 6:18), then neither should we.[3]

Positive Aspects

Positive aspects of unqualified absolutism include the following:

1. It is based on God's unchanging character. A review of previous chapters will remind you that God cannot change; therefore any moral attribute of God can be considered to be absolute as well.
2. It is motivated by the rule rather than by the result. This is in contrast to the relativistic approaches that use an "end justifies the means" mentality. There is integrity and value in an action that is good.
3. It seems logical that if God expects His creatures to be holy, then it would be possible for them to not sin. Why would God tell us not to sin if He knew there would be situations in which we would have to sin? As stated above, according to this view conflicts that do arise are not real

---

[3]Cited in ibid., 85.

but apparent. In other words, one is not truly choosing between moral absolutes but between one absolute and another option that only *seems* to be a moral absolute.

Negative Aspects

Negative aspects of unqualified absolutism include the following:

1. It tends to promote legalism. Always trying to focus on the rightness or wrongness of actions without regard for higher ones could promote the legalistic mindset that Jesus so adamantly preached against.
2. What if honesty and some other moral absolute are in conflict? Which sin is greater, the sin of lying to save a life, or the lack of mercy in allowing a murder or rape? "It was by means of the lie that Rahab's mercy was expressed and the spies were saved. . . . There was no actual separation between the lie and the act of mercy. And a mere formal distinction will not suffice as an explanation, since in actuality there was only one act (which included the lie) under consideration, and this act was praised by God."[4]
3. It cannot be said that every act is evil in and of itself. If this were the case, then when an animal attacks and kills a human it would be an evil act. A dog that steals a bite of food would be sinning. A toddler who plays with a gun and shoots his brother should be held morally responsible, if the act itself is sinful. Yet no reasonable person would accuse the dog or the toddler of sinning. It is not the act but the intent that is either right or wrong. Jesus taught that if one merely *intends* to kill or commit adultery, then one has sinned already, before actually carrying out the evil intentions.
4. A sin of omission can be just as bad as a sin of commission. Lying is a sin of commission. Not preventing the murder or rape of a loved one in your care is a sin of omission. Which is worse? Both are wrong. James 4:17 states, "So whoever knows the right thing to do and fails to do it, for him it is sin." In some situations, to make the

---

[4]Ibid., 89.

choice to do nothing can be just as bad as, if not worse than, the alternative.

5. Jesus, Paul, and many of the disciples faced real moral dilemmas. For instance, Jesus broke the established human interpretation of keeping the Sabbath in order to show mercy (Mark 2:23–27; John 5:5–16).

6. Even Augustine admitted that there are certain divine exceptions to laws, such as when God commanded Abraham to kill his son. Hodge believed that a statement was a lie only "in a context in which the truth is expected."[5] Once exceptions such as these are made, unqualified absolutism begins to look more like graded absolutism, which the next chapter will examine.

7. One cannot always believe that God will spare the faithful. Martyrs, rape victims, and murder victims are the proof of this. Some wrongly interpret 1 Corinthians 10:13, which speaks of God providing a way out of trial, to mean that God will always keep us from moral dilemmas. But such escapes are not always available. Abraham did not know of a third alternative when he chose to obey God and kill his son. The fact that Abraham did not have to follow through with his choice does not negate that he had chosen in his heart to do this deed.

CONCLUSION

The Christian ethic should be adequate for all situations. Situationism is not adequate because of its weak foundation and subjective nature. It is to be commended for its motivation to exalt the virtue of love, but it is unrealistic in its application in various real-life situations due to a lack of objective standards and a lack of a clear definition of love.

Unqualified absolutism also seems inadequate because of apparent real-life conflicts that occur. This approach is to be commended because it is based on the unchanging nature of God and it attempts to resolve all conflicts. However, unquali-

---

[5]Charles Hodge, *Systematic Theology*, 3 vols. (Grand Rapids, Mich.: Eerdmans, 1952), 3:439–444.

fied absolutism is unrealistic because it is unable to provide satisfactory answers for the real moral dilemmas that exist in life.

DISCUSSION/APPLICATION:

1. Discuss the following dilemmas. How should these situations be handled? Don't just answer "yes" or "no," but defend your answers.

   a. You have borrowed a gun from someone who wants it back. You promised that you would return it when you borrowed it. However, your friend is angry and wants it back. You suspect that he might use it to hurt someone. Should you return the gun?

   b. The Hebrew midwives lied in order to save the lives of their babies (see Exodus 1). Telling the truth in this case would not only have resulted in the death of babies, but Moses would not have lived to lead the Israelites out of Egypt. Were these midwives right or wrong?

   c. You see on the news that there is a serial rapist on the loose in your town. You are in your driveway when a strange man approaches you and asks if you have a sister (or wife) in your home. Should you tell this man the truth? By not saying anything or by avoiding the subject you will appear more suspicious to him. Besides lying, what other reasonable options might you have?

2. No Christian would argue with the situationist that love is absolutely right. What other moral ideas could be added to the list of moral absolutes? How is it that the other absolutes can be interpreted as being consistent with love?

3. Try to compare and contrast the four ethical approaches looked at so far in this text. Think of at least one example in the world for each of these approaches.

Chapter 7

ABSOLUTIST ETHICAL SYSTEMS (PART 2)

"EVANGELICALS HAVE GENERALLY held to some form of ethical absolutism. In contrast to situationism, they have claimed that there are many moral absolutes. Within the camp of those holding to two or more absolutes, a special problem arises: What about moral conflicts? What should one do when two or more of his absolute obligations come into unavoidable conflict?"[1]

It is commendable that the unqualified absolutist tries to have a system in which there are no moral conflicts; however, in real life conflicts do arise. These last two approaches honestly allow for conflicts. They differ, however, in how they define these conflicts and in how they respond to them (see Table 7.1).

Table 7.1
Absolutist Ethical Approaches (II)

Conflicting Absolutism	Graded Absolutism
There are many absolutes that sometimes conflict with each other, and it is always wrong to disobey any of them.	There are many absolutes that sometimes conflict with each other, and it is always right to follow the higher law.

---

[1]Norman L. Geisler, *Christian Ethics: Options and Issues* (Grand Rapids, Mich.: Baker, 1989), 97.

CONFLICTING ABSOLUTISM

The conflicting absolutist acknowledges the existence of many absolutes as well as the idea that these absolutes sometimes conflict with each other. The world is in a fallen state as a result of sin. Though it is not God's ideal that humans would find themselves in moral predicaments, such conflicts are part of a temporary curse that will one day be lifted. If and when one of God's children finds himself in such a predicament, he should choose to do the lesser of the two evils and then ask God to forgive him of his sin.

A strength of conflicting absolutism is its realistic view of the reality of moral conflicts. A weakness is that it sometimes views these conflicts as unavoidable absolutes that result in a circumstance in which a person must choose to sin. How could God hold a person accountable for a sin when there was no option of not choosing sin?

GRADED ABSOLUTISM

If moral absolutes flow from the unchanging essence of God, then it follows that moral absolutes would never contradict each other. If they did, then one would have to conclude that there is a contradiction within the nature of God. Yet this is impossible, since God is morally perfect and without contradiction. God's love never conflicts with His holiness. Rather than contradicting each other, God's attributes complement each other. His mercy and grace do not contradict but complement His justice.

God's moral laws do not conflict within His nature; however, in this finite, fallen world, two or more of God's absolute moral laws do sometimes conflict. When that happens, it is our absolute duty to follow the higher law; God exempts us from our duty to the lower one. Here contradiction is not within God but between God and the fallen world in which we live.

For example, the Bible commands people to submit to

the God-ordained human authorities that are in their lives (Rom. 13:1–4; 1 Pet. 2:13). The Bible also commands people to submit to God's holy commands. Problems arise when the God-ordained human authority conflicts with one of God's commands. If a human dictator commands a believer not to pray or read her Bible, the dictator is contradicting these God-ordained commands. The conflict is real. However, the conflict is not between two moral absolutes. It is not a moral absolute to blindly obey every command of every human authority in your life. One should take exception when a human authority conflicts with God.

When there are moral conflicts, the graded absolutist will say that we should obey the greater good or appeal to the higher authority. Is it a greater good to save a person's life or to tell the truth to a potential murderer? The graded absolutist would likely consider it a greater moral responsibility to save the innocent life rather than be honest to a murderer, especially when these two courses of action are in conflict. If the action of being honest to a murderer will result in the death of an innocent person, then one has a responsibility to save the person's life by withholding information from the criminal.

One would not have to ask God for forgiveness for not submitting to a lower authority, since one has not sinned. In the act of disobeying a human authority, one may be obeying God. One should use discernment with this approach and not use God as an excuse not to obey the government. In the areas in which the Scriptures are not clear, one should submit to the human authority.

CONCLUSION

At first glance, conflicting absolutism and graded absolutism may seem like two sides of the same coin. However, it is not as simple as comparing the phrases "lesser of two evils" and "greater good." Both of these approaches acknowledge that there are true moral conflicts in this world. However, these two approaches differ in whether one must sin when making a choice between two conflicting moral actions. Unlike conflicting absolutism, graded absolutism views the person as innocent as long as he or she follows the higher law.

DISCUSSION/APPLICATION:

1. Think of potential conflicts that might arise between the commands of Scripture and the commands of human authorities: parents, police, pastor, president, dictator.
2. How might some people misuse or misunderstand the "do the greater good" approach to ethics?

RECOMMENDED READING

Geisler, Norman L. *Christian Ethics: Options and Issues.* Grand Rapids, Mich.: Baker, 1989.

Chapter 8

FACING THE ISSUES

WHAT WOULD IT BE LIKE to quote John 3:16 to an atheist? An atheist cannot be convinced that God loves him if he does not believe in God. It would be like trying to describe the color of a red rose to someone with red-green color blindness. His perspective is so radically different that he will not understand unless his perspective changes.

The rest of this book (Part 2) will deal with specific ethical issues. This chapter will summarize the theistic approach to ethics and compare it to a naturalistic or secular humanist approach to ethics (see Table 8.1). Biblically, some areas are black and white with no room for disagreement. Other issues are clear in some areas and not so clear in others. These "gray" areas require discernment, prayer, and a spirit of love.

Table 8.1
Theistic and Secular Humanist Worldviews[1]

Theism	Secular Humanism
There is a Creator.	There is no Creator.
Man was specially created.	Man evolved from animals.
God is sovereign over life.	Man is sovereign over life.
Sanctity-of-life principle.	Quality-of-life principle.
End does not justify the means.	End justifies the means.

---

[1]Adapted from Norman L. Geisler, *Christian Ethics: Options and Issues* (Grand Rapids, Mich.: Baker, 1989), 174.

SECULAR HUMANISM

The secular humanist position begins with the presupposition that there is no theistic God. If there is no God, there is no basis for absolute moral truths. Humans are highly evolved animals yet are not morally responsible for their actions. Deviant behavior (behavior outside of what is considered normal in a society) can be corrected by a restructuring of the person's environment, better education, or medical intervention. The secular humanist perspective views ethical issues much differently than does the theistic perspective.

The theistic worldview begins with a belief in a personal, all-powerful, and morally perfect God. As stated in previous chapters, moral ideas that flow from God's nature are absolute. There is a distinct difference between right and wrong. When humans choose to do wrong, it is not simply a result of their genetic makeup or environment. Wrong choices are related to free will and are therefore deserving of punishment.

SANCTITY-OF-LIFE PRINCIPLE

Life has intrinsic value because God created it. Human life especially has intrinsic value because humans are made in God's image. A human life has value whether it is useful or not, whether it is conscious or not, whether it is good or not. According to this principle, a human has value even if he never contributes anything positive to the rest of humanity. Every human being bears the image of God and should be treated with respect.

QUALITY-OF-LIFE PRINCIPLE

The sanctity-of-life principle can be contrasted with the quality-of-life principle of secular humanism. The quality-of-life principle is based on the idea that the quality of one's existence is the pre-eminent factor in making moral choices. For example, a woman may choose whether or not to have an abortion solely on the basis of how that choice would affect the quality of her life—or the quality of life that the unborn child might expect to have. Secular humanists would say that some abortions are justified because the child would be born into a bad home situation. It would be better for him not to be born than to have a bad quality of life. As we go through the issues covered in this book, you will notice how the Christian position consistently emphasizes the sanctity-of-life principle. Sometimes disagreements arise when believers try to apply the sanctity-of-life principle to an issue like war or capital punishment. For example, should the sanctity-of-life principle apply to a criminal or an enemy?

SOVEREIGNTY-OF-GOD PRINCIPLE

The theist believes in a personal God who is sovereign over the universe. This relates to His ability and right to control the universe. In ethics, it means that God is sovereign over life-and-death matters. The secular humanist rejects God and any concept of sovereignty of a higher being. Man is the measure of all things. For all practical purposes, man is God. He can create, destroy, or manipulate life. This point is especially relevant to biomedical issues.

Does the end justify the means? This question is answered "no" by a biblical theist and "yes" by the secular humanist. The humanist says that it is justifiable to destroy some lives in order to improve the quality of or save other lives. The theist leaves life-and-death matters up to God when at all possible. The humanist would be inclined to say that he is pro-cure about human health, but would be willing to use human embryos to achieve this end. Theists would view curing diseases as a positive end but would avoid using human embryos (especially if abortion were involved) in any way to bring about the cure.

CONCLUSION

The two worldviews of secular humanism and biblical theism are in stark contrast to each other. They neither agree philosophically nor agree often on the specific issues in ethics. They come from different perspectives and reach different conclusions. Many people have never taken the time to consider their own perspective and how it influences their decisions in life. It is just as important for a person to know *how* she thinks as it is to know *what* she thinks. The rest of this text will guide you through many issues. Consider your own perspective as you think through and discuss these important issues that humans face in the twenty-first century.

DISCUSSION/APPLICATION:

1. Memorize Table 8.1. Be able to explain each point.
2. Find an article in a major news magazine related to an ethical issue. Read the article and determine whether the article is written from a theistic or a humanistic perspective. List several reasons for your answer.
3. Why might it be an impossible argument for a theist to debate with a secular humanist on the sanctity-of-life principle?
4. The idea of having a proper Christian worldview is becoming more popular in many churches and schools. Though this is a needed emphasis, sometimes popular traditions or political positions get mixed into the definition of a proper Christian worldview. What do you think is a good definition of a Christian worldview? What are things that are sometimes mistaken for being part of a Christian worldview?

THE ISSUES

Chapter 9

LYING

IMAGINE SEEING AN intruder in your home. He puts a gun to your head and demands to know where your mom or some other loved one is located. This loved one happens to be sleeping upstairs. The intruder says he will shoot you if you remain silent. If you tell the truth, you fear that he will kill your loved one. What should you do?

Corrie ten Boom was hiding Jews in her home to protect them from the Nazis during World War II. When the Nazis demanded to know if she was indeed hiding Jews, she lied to save their lives. Did she sin? Would it have been a sin for her to give factual information to the Nazis resulting in the murder of these innocent Jews?

The ethical issue of lying has always been a topic of debate. Some argue that it is never okay to lie. Others argue that lying is not even a matter of right or wrong. The apostle Paul includes the sin of lying in lists of other sins such as murder and drunkenness. Even those who come from the perspective of moral absolutism do not always agree. Part of the controversy relates to the definition of a lie. If one defines a lie as intentional deceit, without qualifying the definition to exclude such things as games or actions within the context of a just war, then one would be forced to admit that lying is sometimes permissible. Thomas Aquinas defined "lie" as a statement at variance with the mind. Augustine took the strict view that the truth should be told whatever the consequences might be.

The ninth commandment of Exodus 20, that one should not "bear false witness," assumes that the person being sinned against is expecting or deserving to know the truth. It is related to being honest under oath in a court of law. To falsely accuse someone or lie to defend a guilty person is a serious injustice. This particular command does not apply to all false statements.

From a biblical perspective, God clearly expects honesty. The New Testament calls lying a sin (Rom. 13:9). Christians should be honest in heart and word. To live a life of lies and deceit is to live a life so far from God that the Bible describes this person as being outside the gates of the city of heaven (Rev. 22:15).

Yet few would take seriously the assertion that deception is always wrong. If there is such a thing as a just war, few would expect nations to be honest and forthright with their military strategies. Playing a game of cards or chess often requires intentional deceit in order to win. Many plays in sports are designed to deceive the opponent. It would be ridiculous to categorize games or sports as sinful based on a nonbiblical definition of a lie.

What is a biblical, commonsense definition of a lie? In general, a lie is the intent to deceive someone. Some would qualify this by adding, "deceiving those who deserve or expect to know the truth." This definition takes into consideration that telling the truth may actually sometimes bring one into conflict with a higher moral principle. It says that people should be honest in their everyday conversations with friends and enemies alike. But it allows for deception in things like sporting events or games in which the opponents are not expecting the truth. It allows for deception in the case of a just war against an enemy that neither expects nor deserves the truth to be told—because of the higher law that says we should protect the innocent. An intruder in your home does not deserve to know where your children are hiding or where you keep valuables. One would not necessarily have to give false information to this intruder. Calling the police, maintaining silence, or employing physical resistance may be options. However, in the event that there are no other options, some theists believe that deception would be permissible in order to save a life. The graded absolutist would say that to be honest to a criminal is a lower priority than saving the life of an innocent person. The loving thing, and therefore the right thing to do, would be to save the innocent life.

The unqualified absolutist might disagree. He might say one should either appeal to one of the other options or tell the truth and leave the results up to God. One would not sin in so doing, since God is sovereign and has allowed this event to take place. The graded absolutist might say that one has sinned by not saving the life.

ABSOLUTE TRUTH

One may think that the whole issue of lying has been dealt with rather lightly; however, it is important to establish an accurate definition of a lie rather than oversimplify the issue by defining a lie as mere deception. Likewise, it is important to define truth: truth is that which corresponds to reality. What is real is what is true. Facts are true regardless of people's opinion about the circumstances or their relation to the circumstances. The statement "two plus two equals four" is true whether a person agrees with it or not. Truth is narrow. There are an infinite number of possible answers to this math equation, but there is only one correct answer. There are many possibilities about where you *could* be as you read this paragraph, but there is only one place where you *actually* are at any given time. If you are sitting in a chair in a classroom, then it is *true* that you are sitting in that chair.

Another way to illustrate the nature of truth is by the law of noncontradiction. This law of logic states that opposite ideas cannot both be true at the same time and in the same sense.[1] The opposite of what is true is false. If something is up in one sense, it is not down in that same sense. If something is wrong in one sense, it is not right in that same sense. Humans did not invent the law of noncontradiction. We only discovered and described it. It is what it is. Any person who attempts to disprove the law of noncontradiction will be forced to use language and a form of reasoning that assumes the law of noncontradiction. For example, if I say, "The law of noncontradiction does not apply to all statements," I imply that it does, because I don't believe that the opposite of that statement can be true.

RELATIVISM

The alternative to an absolute view of truth is relativism. Relativism is the idea that truth changes depending on circumstances. Even though people try to live by a relativistic morality, it is impossible to live by it consistently. For the very things they do, they do not want others to do to them. Their actions toward others are inconsistent with their expectations of others.

CONCLUSION

It is morally wrong to intend to deceive someone who deserves or expects to know the truth. The following exercises will help you think through this issue. A relativist's approach to lying fails because truth corresponds to what is real. And not everything can be true but only what corresponds to reality. What does not correspond to reality is false. If there is a God, then it can be said that God is real. Those things that are known about Him are also real. These things we know about God that are true

---

[1]What we mean by "in the same sense" can be illustrated by the following example. Suppose that John is standing in his front yard talking to a friend on his cell phone when the friend asks where John is. If John replies, "inside," he is lying if he intends his friend to believe that he is inside the house. If his friend would drive by and see John in the yard, he would assume that John had lied. Of course, John might try to appear innocent and say, "I meant 'inside' in the sense that I was inside the boundary of my property." In examining truth claims, it is important to know the "sense" of the claim being made.

will form the basis of morality. It is important to tell the truth. Regardless of whether you end up taking the graded absolutist or the unqualified absolutist position on lying, it is important to highly regard honesty and avoid the sin of lying. Lying as such is always wrong. Only when there is a higher moral law (such as showing mercy to the innocent) are we exempt from our lower duty of telling the truth—so that we can fulfill our obligation to the higher duty.

DISCUSSION/APPLICATION:

1. Refute the following relative truth claims by applying the claim to itself:
    a. There are no absolutes.
    b. Truth is relative.
    c. No person or religion has the truth.
    d. That's just your interpretation.
    e. You should not judge.
2. Do a study of the word "truth" in the Bible using concordances, Bible dictionaries, and online and/or Bible software resources.
3. Reflect on the following six ethical approaches viewed in previous chapters as they apply to the particular issue of lying. Fill in the name of the particular ethical approach that fits best with the statement on lying:
    a. _____ Lying is neither right nor wrong.
    b. _____ Lying is generally wrong.
    c. _____ Lying is sometimes right if it is the loving thing to do.
    d. _____ Lying is always wrong.
    e. _____ Lying is forgivable.
    f. _____ Lying is sometimes right, when it is for the greater good.
4. Graded absolutists cite certain examples from the Bible in which lying was an acceptable option. Read the passages and then share your thoughts about these scenarios:

a. Shiphrah and Puah, two Hebrew midwives, were dishonest to the Pharaoh in order to save the lives of baby boys (Ex. 1:15–21).

b. Jonathan was dishonest to King Saul in order to protect the life of his friend David (1 Samuel 19–20).

c. Rahab was dishonest in order to protect the lives of Jewish spies (Joshua 2). She was commended for her faith in God, according to Hebrews 11:31. Can her faith be separated from her action?

Chapter 10

CHEATING

A HIGH SCHOOL STUDENT, John, copied and pasted an article on euthanasia from the Internet for an ethics paper. The paper was worth two test grades. If he were caught, he would receive two zeros and likely fail the semester. The teacher, Mr. Skinner, knew John's typical work and was suspicious of plagiarism. A quick search on the Internet confirmed Mr. Skinner's suspicion. Instead of confronting John directly, the teacher saw this as an opportunity to teach him a lesson. Mr. Skinner announced before the class that someone was guilty of plagiarism and would be receiving two zeros and disciplinary action unless he would come forward after class within the next three days and admit his guilt privately to the teacher. Mr. Skinner planned to let John redo his paper for half credit. Three days later, to Mr. Skinner's surprise, eight students out of a class of fifty had come forward admitting that they might have cheated. John was not one of the eight.

This true story (with names changed to protect both the innocent and the guilty) is not an isolated incident but an everyday occurrence in high schools and colleges everywhere. Most students have cheated at some point during their educational career. Some students do it so often and are so good at it that they depend on cheating to get them to graduation. Reasons students give for cheating in school include:

1. So many other students are cheating that, if I don't, I will not be able to compete with them academically.
2. I don't like this required subject; whatever I do in life will have nothing to do with this subject. I might as well cheat to get through it.
3. The consequences of failing this class (or getting a low passing grade) are so great that I must cheat.
4. I don't have time to do all the work in all my classes. I have to cheat on a few or I will never get everything done.

Whatever the justification one gives for cheating, it is still dishonest. It is a form of lying; it is also a form of stealing when students obtain papers or answers from sources not their own. There are several practical reasons for students to think twice before cheating:

1. Education is expensive. When one resorts to cheating, he is cheating his parents or himself of the money spent to attain knowledge.
2. When one cheats, one cheats himself of the joy of learning and possessing knowledge that would enrich his life.
3. A grade in a class that is the result of cheating is not the same as earning the grade. There will likely be guilt and regret later on for not having worked hard to earn the grade.
4. Cheating in high school creates a pattern and habit that is difficult to break. It becomes a lifestyle for some that destroys careers and families.
5. Though many students do not get caught right away, many do eventually get caught. A consequence of getting caught is usually automatic failure of the course. Most institutions of higher learning will automatically dismiss a student from school for cheating. Cheating is forgivable; however, the shame of being dismissed from an institution for cheating is something a person will have to live with the rest of his life.

There are also several spiritual reasons to think twice before cheating:

1. Cheating is dishonest, and therefore sinful. It is disobedience to God; like other sins, it hurts a person's walk with the Lord.
2. "Be sure your sin will find you out" (Num. 32:23). Some cheaters seem never to get caught. However, this precept from the Bible indicates that the sin will eventually catch up with the sinner. You reap what you sow. A person may get away with stealing, lying, or cheating sometimes. However, the Scriptures imply that if one continues in a particular sin, the sin will find him out.
3. A clean conscience before God brings more contentment than earthly success. "Now there is great gain in godliness with contentment" (1 Tim. 6:6). Solomon hated his life at one point despite his incredible wealth, power, and notoriety. His problem was that he had strayed from God in his heart (Ecclesiastes 2–3).
4. It is not God's will for your life to gain anything by cheating. If you get into a college only because you cheated to get there, it is not God's will for you to be in that college. Cheating on your taxes will result in your having money that God did not intend for you to have.

CONCLUSION

Cheating is wrong. Most people instinctively know this, but some try to rationalize their dishonesty. The practical and spiritual considerations given prove that cheating is not worth the risks involved. Now is the time to determine that cheating is not going to be a way of life for you.

DISCUSSION/APPLICATION:

1. Look at the following scenarios and determine whether these involve cheating:
   a. Students share answers on a homework assignment.

    b. The teacher assigns a group project and one person does all of the work.

    c. Something outside the window informs a person of the correct answer on the test.

    d. A teacher gives an open-note test. A student who did not take notes looks at another student's notes during the test.

    e. A parent helps you with your homework.

2. Cheating in high school creates a pattern and habit that is difficult to break. List or discuss some of the ways in which cheating becomes a lifestyle and how it can prove destructive later in life.

3. Consider how those who do honest work must feel when students around them are cheating and getting better grades.

Chapter 11

STEALING

IMAGINE WALKING DOWN a sidewalk and noticing a wallet on a bench. No one is sitting there. No one seems to be looking for anything. You decide to sit on the bench. You wait. No one approaches. You pick up the wallet to look for a name so that you can be a good Samaritan and you are shocked by the thickness of the wallet. It is full of cash—mostly $100 bills. You also notice from the driver's license that the owner is from out of state and is probably on vacation. Of course, he could also be a drug dealer. Your first instinct is to keep it, thinking that no one will ever know—and you need the money. Maybe this is God's way of getting it to you. Then you consider calling the police or turning it in to a nearby store clerk. But your distrust of people in general causes you to hesitate. What do you do?

Imagine coming home from vacation to find the glass in one of your windows shattered. You walk in the house and see drawers pulled out with the contents strewn across the floor. Your laptop is gone. So is a big part of your CD and DVD collection. You wonder what else is missing. You have a sickening feeling of having been wronged. Your private space was ravaged. You no longer feel secure in the one place where you thought you were safe.

Stealing is a sin. It is even on God's "top ten list" in Exodus 20. It comes in many forms. When someone steals from you, it hurts. It is easy to associate bank robberies or convenience store holdups with stealing. Stealing happens in the corporate world when executives embezzle money or don't pay taxes. Stealing happens when a child puts a pack of bubble gum in his pocket even though he knows his parents should pay for it. Of course the consequences are greater for stealing millions than for stealing a dollar; however, it is the principle of stealing that makes it wrong, not the amount stolen.

STEALING IS WRONG

The Bible clearly teaches that stealing is wrong. The Old Testament associates stealing with dishonesty (Lev. 19:11). It is also listed with sins such as murder, adultery, and idolatry (Jer. 7:9). In the New Testament, Jesus affirms the sinfulness of stealing by listing it along with some of the other Ten Commandments (Matt. 19:18). So does Paul in Romans 13:9.

Besides biblical evidence, the law in almost every culture throughout history has consistently viewed stealing as wrong. Some cultures have even advocated cutting off the hand of a thief. C. S. Lewis has an appendix in the back of his book *The Abolition of Man* in which he lists various statements from ancient writings and religions throughout the world. Lewis references the Babylonian Talmud and ancient Egyptian writings, as well as ancient Jewish and Greek writings that condemn stealing.[1] His point is to support the existence of a universal moral law. Apparently, stealing is part of that law.

WHY STEALING IS WRONG

Stealing is wrong, but why is it wrong, other than being an offense to the character of God? Perhaps the most basic reason that stealing is wrong is that it is unloving to the person you stole from. It in some way hurts the one who was stolen from. This point needs no explanation to anyone who has been violated by a thief. Just ask someone who has had his car stolen

---

[1]C. S. Lewis, *The Abolition of Man* (San Francisco: HarperSanFrancisco, 1974), 93. First published in 1944.

or house invaded. Though one pack of gum may not in and of itself hurt the owner of a convenience store, the cumulative cost of many people stealing over time is high enough that it hurts the business owner. He must invest in security cameras and raise prices. This then hurts everyone who buys from him.

Consumers are hit especially hard when it comes to property insurance. Insurance fraud is when someone dishonestly reports damage or other loss to an insurance company in order to collect a payment. The cost of insurance fraud has been estimated to be as high as eighty billion dollars annually.[2] Everyone's insurance premiums go up because of the small percentage of people who steal in this way.

Stealing is also wrong because God desires that people work for their living. Ephesians 4:28 states, "Let the thief no longer steal, but rather let him labor, doing honest work with his own hands, so that he may have something to share with anyone in need." It is selfish to steal. It is better to work so that you can have an abundance of things to share with others.

Perhaps one of the most common forms of stealing in contemporary culture is related to information and entertainment. These include activities such as illegal downloading of music or movies, illegal copying of software or video games, and copyright infringement. Some people claim ignorance; however, if there is a copyright symbol (©) on the product, then it is considered stealing to make copies without permission. The specifics of the law vary depending on the types of media. With books, it is permissible to quote from the text as long as the original source is cited appropriately, such as with the footnotes in a book. It is sometimes permissible to use short clips from a film when putting together presentations. It is important to check the specifics of the law before doing this. It is never permissible to make copies of CDs or DVDs and distribute or sell them

---

[2]Coalition against Insurance Fraud, "Top Thirteen Insurance Swindlers Enter Insurance Fraud Hall of Shame," http://www.insurancefraud.org/releases_2002.htm (accessed October 21, 2006).

unless you own the rights to that product. Making a copy of a movie borrowed from a friend so that you do not have to buy it does not arouse the same emotions as does a car theft or a house being robbed, but it is still a form of stealing.

CONCLUSION

Stealing is a sin, even though it is very common and sometimes easy to do. The Bible speaks clearly to this issue. The moral law also speaks clearly on this issue. Stealing hurts not only the person or business robbed—everyone pays for it. Even if copying information with technology does not seem to hurt anyone, it is a form of dishonesty and will jeopardize one's relationship with God.

DISCUSSION/APPLICATION:

1. Is it really stealing if the person or company has so much that he/it will never notice that something is missing? Defend your answer.
2. What keeps you from stealing? Is it the fear of getting caught? Is it more?
3. The story about the lost wallet at the beginning of the chapter is based on a true story that one of the authors of this book encountered. What would be the best option for getting the wallet back to its rightful owner? Discuss the following options and try to apply the Golden Rule by imagining that it was your wallet that was lost. How would you want it to be handled?
   a. Immediately call the police.
   b. Turn the wallet in to the nearest store clerk or manager.
   c. Take the wallet home and write a letter to the individual named on the driver's license.
   d. Wait around a few minutes for the owner to return looking for it.
   e. Other.

Chapter 12

CIVIL DISOBEDIENCE

SHOULD CHRISTIANS EVER disobey the government? What if you were drafted to fight in a war you believed was morally wrong? What if you and your spouse were expecting your third child and you lived in a society that forced abortions after the second child to prevent overpopulation? Of the three basic approaches to this issue, two acknowledge the God-ordained authority of government in a spirit of submission. The third, anarchism, is not held by many. It claims that one is never required to obey the government. But this approach is not practical; it would never work in the "real world." No society can afford to allow its citizens to disregard the authority of government. The other two approaches will be looked at more closely in this chapter.

RADICAL PATRIOTISM

The radical patriot believes that one should submit to the government at all times. They attempt to find biblical justification for this position in Romans 13:1–4, which states that human governments are ordained by God; whoever resists these ordained powers is resisting God. It is interesting that Paul probably wrote this while Nero was emperor of Rome. Nero was an evil ruler who killed his own mother to ascend to the throne and persecuted and killed multitudes of Christians. Titus 3:1 also reminds people to obey the civil authorities over them, as does 1 Peter 2:13.

Radical patriotism says we should be obedient even to an evil government. God will not hold the individual accountable for the evil choices of those in power. It is possible that God is using the wickedness of one nation to judge the wickedness of another. This was often the case in the Old Testament when God used evil pagan nations to judge the sins of the nation of Israel.

The Christian patriot equates submission to government with submission to God. His motto is "My country, right or wrong."

BIBLICAL SUBMISSIONISM

The biblical submissionist would emphatically state that Christians have the right to disobey their government when it promotes or demands an action that is contrary to the Bible. The law of God is absolute; it is higher than the law of man. Blind allegiance to a government could be a form of idolatry. One is required to obey a government to the extent that it is under God. In areas of conflict, one must obey God. But this should be done in a spirit of submission to God rather than out of rebellion against human authority.

Biblical submissionists disagree about where to draw the line on civil disobedience. One approach is to disobey the government only when laws *compel* people to do evil. People holding to this position would say that it is wrong to disobey the government in order to protest abortion. It would be wrong because the government is in this case merely allowing an evil to occur, not forcing people to have abortions. Oppressive governments sometimes compel people to do evil. It would be permissible to disobey these governments. This approach is drawn from the biblical examples that approve of disobedience to oppressive governments (Exodus 5; Daniel 3, 6; Acts 4; Revelation 13). The rule here is that we should always obey government when it takes its place *under* God (Rom. 13:1–4), but never when it takes the place *of* God.

Another approach asserts that one has the right to disobey laws that *permit* actions contrary to the Bible. For example, a person could actually try to use force to stop an abortion from taking place. Biblically, an individual cannot justify using violence against abortion doctors or others in authority who are committing evil acts. However, a government does have the right to enforce laws against abortions, and therefore it could be argued that Christians are best off working to educate people and influence governments to protect innocent lives.

A person contemplating disobedience of laws should obey the following guidelines:

1. Make sure there is a biblical reason for your actions.
2. Disobey peacefully.
3. Keep in mind that it is permissible to flee a nation that is promoting an evil.
4. Be willing to accept the consequences of disobedience.
5. Remember that resistance can involve active spiritual, moral, and political efforts.

CONCLUSION

Anarchism approves of civil disobedience at any time. Radical patriotism forbids civil disobedience for any reason. Biblical submissionism allows for civil disobedience sometimes, but there is disagreement about when disobedience is justified. The heart of the believer should always be one of submission to God and to government. When one finds God's law and the government's law in conflict, one should obey the absolute law of God rather than the law of man.

DISCUSSION/APPLICATION:

1. Do you think that blind loyalty to American policy (wars, economic policies, etc.) is a form of radical patriotism?

2. Should states have the right to resist federal laws when they are in conflict with the Bible? For instance, if the federal government required states to use curriculum in public schools that promotes a humanistic, unbiblical philosophy, while not allowing intelligent design to be taught alongside evolution, should states have the right to disobey and allow its schools to teach intelligent design?

3. Was the American Revolution a just act of civil disobedience or was it an example of sinful rebellion?

Chapter 13

ECONOMIC
INJUSTICE

MEDIAN HOUSEHOLD INCOME WAS $44,000 in 2004 in the United States, but that doesn't mean that everyone enjoyed that level of economic well-being. Some thirty-seven million people were living below the "poverty line" of $15,067 income for a household of three.[1] And nearly forty-six million people, many of them with otherwise adequate income, were without health insurance. On the other end of the spectrum, in 2005 there were about nine million households with a net worth of one million dollars or greater.[2]

While it is not a sin to be rich (Abraham and Job were), it is wrong not to help the poor. Indeed, it is necessary for own-ers of large businesses (who, after all, provide many jobs for poorer people) to have enough wealth in order to make large investments in their businesses. Again, however, it is wrong to oppress the poor. The net worth of certain American billionaires is more than the gross domestic product of some small nations. Should the government force those with the most wealth to give some of their wealth to feed, clothe, house, and provide health care to the poor? Should there be a "maximum wage

---

[1]U.S. Census Bureau, "Income, Poverty, and Health Insurance Coverage in the United States: 2004," http://www.census.gov/hhes/www/poverty/poverty04.html.
[2]Jeanne Sahadi, "Number of Millionaires Hits Record," *CNNMoney.com*, http://www.cnn.com/2005/09/28/news/economy/millionaire_survey/ (posted September 28, 2005).

law" that would require all income over a certain amount to be used to help the poor?

Those with higher incomes already pay a higher percentage of taxes than people with lower incomes, and much of this money is redistributed by the federal government to help the poor with various welfare and medical aid. Some advocate taxing the rich even more; others believe that this would hurt the economy by making less money available for business owners to hire new employees. Furthermore, by penalizing people who make more, those people might be discouraged from working harder to increase their productivity and their incomes. It could also breed laziness in those who find that they can get a check from the government every month without having to work.

While the political debates rage on, Christians should look to the Bible for wisdom. References to poverty and how to treat poor people are too numerous to include a complete list in this chapter. The following passages summarize some of the principles that reflect a biblical view regarding poverty.

Jesus lived a life of poverty. Paul taught that a man must provide for his family or he is "worse than an unbeliever" (1 Tim. 5:8). Jesus taught that those who feed, clothe, and house the poor are indirectly serving Him, while those who do not minister to the poor are in danger of judgment (Matt. 25:34–40). David taught that a righteous person shows mercy and gives (Ps. 37:21). The apostle John wrote, "But if anyone has the world's goods and sees his brother in need, yet closes his heart against him, how does God's love abide in him?" (1 John 3:17). Proverbs 19:17 states, "Whoever is generous to the poor lends to the LORD, and he will repay him for his deed." The way Christians respond to the needs of the poor is a good measure of their relationship with God (Prov. 14:21, 31; 17:5; 21:13; 28:27; 31:20). To make yourself rich at a poor person's expense is wrong (Prov. 22:16, 22–23). There is even a prohibition in the Mosaic law against charging interest on loans made to the poor (Ex. 22:25; Lev. 25:35–37). God will repay generous deeds (Prov. 28:8).

The Old Testament Law provided social arrangements to help the poor by allowing them to glean leftovers in the field (Lev. 19:9–10; 23:22; Deut. 24:19–20). In New Testament times, deacons were to help the poor and needy (Acts 6:1–6). A portion of church offerings should be used for the poor and for fellow Christians who may be experiencing hardships (Deut. 14:28–29; Rom. 15:25–27; 1 Cor. 16:1–2).

COMMON OBJECTIONS TO HELPING THE POOR

1. "Giving to the poor will encourage them to be lazy."

It is true that some people are lazy. A good steward will take this into consideration when giving to individuals. However, many find themselves in hardships that are beyond their control. And, giving to people in need who are willing to work (1 Thess. 4:11) may open up a door to minister to them and actually help them to help themselves.

2. "People can be healed physically, fed, and clothed, and still die without Christ."

Of all people, Jesus would have known this, yet He spent much of His public ministry living with and ministering to the poor. He also repeatedly taught that the poor should be ministered to (Matt. 25:34–40; Luke 3:11). Sometimes people will not respond to their important spiritual needs until they have their other needs met.

3. "The Bible says that the poor will always be with us" (Matt. 26:11).

This is true. Perhaps this is part of God's plan so that those who have the means to help others will have ample opportunities to do so. This passage in no way teaches that, since the poor will always be with us, they should not be helped. It is a quote from Deuteronomy 15:11, which is found in a context in which debts for the poor are cancelled every seven years. This statement may be a hard reality, but it is not the ideal. The ideal was stated earlier in the chapter: "But there will be no poor among you" (Deut. 15:4).

4. "People who work hard have earned their money."

Perhaps people who work hard have earned the right to do with some of their income as they see fit. Yet we must remember that everything in heaven and on earth belongs to God (Ps. 24:1). Everything we have has been given to us by God, including money and talents as well as job and educational opportunities. Giving a portion back to Him and to others is more than reasonable.

It is also true that there are some people who work very hard but remain poor. Perhaps these individuals lost good jobs or live in a weak economic region. Even in the United States, there are widowed young mothers who have to choose between caring for their children and working. Either way, finances are tight.

Each of the objections can be answered with the fact that God has commanded believers to give to the poor.

HOW TO HELP

Many Christians are quick to point out that nowhere does the Bible mandate forced giving to the poor. However, the preceding references build a strong case that true believers should not have to be coerced in this area. Those who have more should give abundantly with a thankful heart to God and with a compassionate heart to those in need. Though giving should not be done for personal gain, God promises a blessing for those who give. Here are a few suggestions about how you as an individual can make a difference by helping the poor:

1. Be responsible with the money that God has given you. Good stewardship will give you and your family security and will enable you to give more to others.
2. Be sensitive to the needs of those around you. When you see a need, consider how you could help. Remember that there are ways other than money by which to help people.
3. Give to organizations and ministries that specialize in bringing relief to the poor.
4. Volunteer for an organization that specializes in helping the poor.
5. Suggest ways to your pastor that your church can combine giving to the poor with reaching them with the gospel.

CONCLUSION

Helping the poor is the right thing to do because it involves putting into action moral absolutes based on God's unchanging nature. God is just and loving. The economic disparity among mankind is a type of social injustice. This is not to say that everyone must have the same amount of wealth. The Bible does not directly support or defend any type of political or economic system. The Bible encourages people to live a life of love and generosity regarding their fellow man.

DISCUSSION/APPLICATION:

1. Organize a group to visit a local soup kitchen or homeless shelter.
2. Do you think that poverty is an ethical issue that should carry as much weight in deciding whom to vote for as other moral issues such as abortion?
3. What political issues are affected by the reality of poverty?
4. How can you help the poor without being a bad steward?
5. How does your church help the poor?

Chapter 14

HOMOSEXUAL SIN

NO ISSUE IS MORE CONTROVERSIAL in American society today than the issue of homosexuality. Much of the stigma associated with this lifestyle has been exaggerated by individuals who make fun of or use violence against homosexuals. Homosexuals have been labeled as insane or guilty of an unpardonable sin. On the other extreme, there are militant gays who desire to impose their values on the rest of society through the public educational system and popular media.

Is homosexuality a choice, or is it related to an orientation embedded in the genetic makeup of an individual? What provisions, if any, should a society make to recognize the homosexual lifestyle? Should businesses be required to extend health care benefits to their gay employees and their partners in the same way as they do to married heterosexual couples? Some states recognize same-sex unions. Should states be required to recognize homosexual "marriages" with all the privileges afforded to heterosexual married couples, including the right to adopt children?

The Bible includes numerous passages relating to homosexuality, none of which present it in a positive light. However, those homosexuals who claim to be Christians explain these passages of Scriptures in various other ways.

PRO-GAY POSITIONS

1. Sexual tendencies are inherited. Being gay is not a choice. Most people in the homosexual community will claim that their lifestyle is based on the way they were born. Homosexuals claim that to try to be "straight" would be as strange to them as trying to be gay would be to straight people. They could no more change being gay than they could change the color of their eyes or skin.

2. People should be able to do whatever they want in private. They should simply be left alone as long as they are not hurting anyone. It is argued that the heterosexual majority should not impose their lifestyle on the homosexual minority.

3. The public education system should be more aggressive in promoting gay rights and presenting gay relationships as a normal alternative lifestyle.

4. A loving mutual relationship between two human beings should not be regulated by society or insulted by religious groups. Gays should be allowed to express their love for each other in the same way that heterosexuals do, such as in marriage.

5. Gay couples should be allowed to adopt children. A loving home is a loving home, regardless of the type of relationship those within the home have with each other.

6. Isaiah 56:3-5 (regarding eunuchs in the messianic kingdom) is a prophecy that there will be homosexuals in the church.

7. There may be gay relationships approved of in the Bible, such as David and Jonathan (1 Samuel 18–20).

RESPONSES TO PRO-GAY POSITIONS

1. The homosexual lifestyle is a choice. Despite years of research, geneticists have yet to prove that there is a "gay gene." There are some men who have lower testosterone levels than other men, and women who have higher levels than other women. This could be one of many contributing factors for some who choose to practice homosexuality. However, the bottom line is that regardless of

one's desires, actions are related to one's choices. It is difficult to imagine a society in which everyone acted out every impulse or desire they had. Violence, molestation, theft, and other serious crimes would be out of control. To some degree, every responsible human exercises a level of self-control. A desire does not justify an action. This is true for heterosexuals and homosexuals alike.

2. Any type of sex education curriculum should not promote the homosexual lifestyle without including the facts about health risks associated with this lifestyle. The idea that people should be able to do what they want as long as they are not hurting anyone should include the fact that gays might be hurting themselves as well as family members and friends who love them. A right to privacy does not give someone a right to commit any immoral act. Likewise, mutual consent between adults does not justify an action that is biblically defined as immoral.

3. The homosexual lifestyle is unhealthy. It increases the risk of AIDS, colon and rectal cancer, and hepatitis.[1] The male homosexual lifestyle shortens the lifespan by more than two decades, even for those who do not have AIDS.[2] Some homosexuals might resent the publishing of these facts, but if the facts are true they should be made known. Smokers have a right to know that smoking can compromise their health. In a spirit of love, homosexuals should also be informed of these facts.

4. Any society has the right to regulate behavior that is damaging to human health. Other examples of such worthwhile regulation in American society include laws regarding drug use, the wearing of seatbelts, and driving under the influence of alcohol.

5. The biblical institution of marriage involves one woman with one man (Gen. 2:24). Any aberration from this is not God's ideal. Having both genders in the home for

---

[1]Jeffrey Satinover, *Homosexuality and the Politics of Truth* (Grand Rapids, Mich.: Baker, 1996), 51.

[2]Paul Cameron, William Playfair, and Stephen Wellum, "The Longevity of Homosexuals: Before and After the AIDS Epidemic," *Omega Journal of Death and Dying* 29, no. 3 (1994): 249–272.

children to learn from will help them understand and appreciate both genders when they become adults.

6. The eunuchs of Isaiah 56:3-5 were not homosexual. If anything, a eunuch could be thought of as asexual, not homosexual. Even in the church age, there are men who have a special gift of being single. These are probably men who do not have a strong sexual desire for anyone. These men are a type of "spiritual eunuch."

7. Only reading a pro-gay agenda into the text will result in seeing a gay relationship between David and Jonathan. David had several wives. There is nothing in the Bible to prove that anything other than a close friendship existed between these two men. In fact there is no known gay relationship recorded in Scripture that was written of in an approving manner. On the other hand, there are numerous references to homosexuality presented in a disapproving manner.

BIBLICAL REFERENCES

1. God ordained a specific form of heterosexuality when He created mankind. God created male and female. Genesis 2:24 states, "Therefore a man shall leave his father and his mother and hold fast to his wife, and they shall become one flesh." The writer of Hebrews states, "Let marriage be held in honor among all, and let the marriage bed be undefiled, for God will judge the sexually immoral and adulterous" (Heb. 13:4).

2. The famous story about the destruction of Sodom and Gomorrah is one that inspired the word "sodomy" to describe a homosexual act. There were men in the city who wanted to engage in sexual acts with the men of God who were sent to warn Lot of the coming destruction. These men of God were actually angels in disguise, and they responded to these men by blinding their eyes. What these men wanted to do was sinful, and they were judged accordingly. However, contrary to popular interpretation, the sin of Sodom is not clearly defined in the text as being related only to homosexuality. When God first

told Abraham of the imminent destruction, He simply described the sin as very grave (Gen. 18:20). Jude 7 does indicate that their sin was related to sexual immorality. Homosexual sin was likely part of though not the only reason for the incredible judgment of fire and brimstone on Sodom and Gomorrah (see Ezek. 16:49).

3. The Mosaic law described homosexual sin as a capital crime. Leviticus 18:22 calls the act of two men lying with each other detestable. Some attempt to remove this passage from the list of those that can be used against homosexual sin, since it was part of the Old Testament Law. Few would suggest that a homosexual act between consenting adults should be a capital crime today; however, the fact that it *was* a capital crime under the Law should indicate the severity of this sin in the eyes of the writers of the Old Testament.

4. Romans 1:24–27 describes homosexuality among pagans as sinful desire, sexual impurity, degrading, unnatural, shameful, indecent, and perverse. Paul includes this in the context of a passage that deals with other sins such as idolatry and pride. Some have tried to use this passage to indicate that homosexual sin is worse than all other sin. This approach comes across as arrogant and self-righteous and does little to bring repentance and healing in the gay community. This passage clearly speaks against homosexual sin. It does not label it as categorically worse than the other sins. In fact, as just indicated, the reference to homosexual sin is followed by a lengthy list of other sins (vv. 28–32). Christians should remember to acknowledge their own sins rather than being so quick to point out the sins of others.

5. First Corinthians 6:9b–10 states that "neither the sexually immoral, nor idolaters, nor adulterers, nor men who practice homosexuality, nor thieves, nor the greedy, nor drunkards, nor revilers, nor swindlers will inherit the kingdom of God." Paul points out that some of the Corinthians had the same struggles. Since their conversion to Christ, there was an expectation that they no

longer practiced these sins. Once again, homosexual sin is included in a list with other sins.

A CHRISTIAN RESPONSE

Christians must continue to grapple with some of the questions asked earlier in this chapter. Though many churches and other organizations are doing things to help bring healing to homosexuals, more progress is needed.

The Bible condemns homosexual sin. Homosexuality is a perversion of God's gift of sex. This text cannot begin to exhaust all the arguments on either side of the debate; however, sufficient evidence has been given to prove the biblical point of view about whether homosexuality is right or wrong. Christians must realize that homosexual behavior is a very real temptation to many who need the love of Christ. Making fun of people in the gay community will only push people away from Christ and force them to look elsewhere for love and acceptance. It may reinforce a mistaken notion that there is no real love in the church. Nowhere today is the idea that we should "hate the sin but love the sinner" more important than in how we relate to the homosexual community.

DISCUSSION/APPLICATION:

1. How can people apply the principle of speaking the truth in love to their dealings with the homosexual community?
2. Why do you think some people view homosexual sin as worse than other sexual sins?
3. Suppose one of your close friends told you that he or she was beginning to have thoughts of being gay. How would you handle this?

RECOMMENDED READING

Geisler, Norman L., and Frank Turek. *Legislating Morality: Is It Wise? Is It Legal? Is It Possible?* Minneapolis: Bethany House, 1989.

Chapter 15

HETEROSEXUAL SIN

IN NORWAY, AS MANY AS 80 percent of firstborn children are born out of wedlock.[1] More people than ever are going against more than five thousand years of human history and tradition by practicing cohabitation rather than marriage.

Human sexuality has been a controversial and sometimes confusing issue for many since the beginning of civilization. Many people question the narrow biblical standard of limiting sex to a marriage relationship. Judging by the media and pop culture, it seems that very few people agree with the traditional standard. Actually, there are still many people who choose to live according to biblical standards in this area. More important than what many people believe or how they choose to live is the ethical idea of what is right. A good step toward finding what is right is determining the biblical purposes of sexuality.

THE PURPOSES OF SEX

Procreation

When God created the first two humans, He created a male and a female. He commanded them to "be fruitful and multiply and fill the earth" (Gen. 1:28). The most basic purpose of sex

---

[1]Stanley Kurtz, "Death of Marriage in Scandinavia," *Boston Globe*, March 10, 2004, A23.

is procreation or reproduction. God created the best scenario for raising children in a family that has both a mother and a father. Due to divorce or death, this ideal is not always possible. Death cannot be avoided. Sometimes divorce is inevitable. Yet the most devastating cause for the breakdown of the traditional family and the leading cause of divorce relates to unbiblical sexual practices.

No other expression of sexuality is conducive to creating the ideal environment for raising a family. Deviant expressions of sexuality have led to the births of many unwanted children as well as many abortions. Children in broken homes often have a more difficult time adjusting socially at school, at work, and in their own future marriages.

Pleasure

The Song of Solomon portrays the beauty of human sexuality and the pleasure associated with a marriage relationship. God created sex; humans should not feel guilty for having sex within the boundaries of marriage. Some Christians have condemned sex as a necessary evil; some have even blamed the sin of Adam and Eve on sex. There is no biblical justification for either of these points. In fact, the writer of Hebrews says that the marriage bed can be undefiled (Heb. 13:4), meaning that it is (ideally) a place of innocence.

Prefigure

The ideal marriage is a prefigure or foreshadow of the relationship between Christ and the church (Eph. 5:32). There should be no adultery or love affair with people outside of the marriage relationship, just as there should not be worship of other gods or idols in our Christian walk. Just as one's spouse should be the only object of sexual desire in a marriage, God should be the only object of spiritual desire in life.

Sex allows a husband and a wife a level of intimacy that

they do not share (or should not share) with any other human being. One cannot fully express this open intimacy if one of the spouses is not being true to his or her partner. The breakdown of trust in any area creates a wedge in a marriage that often will lead to a complete disunion.

Likewise the believer's relationship with God should be on a unique level of spiritual intimacy. Trust and a level of devotion unrivaled by other spiritual forces or things of this world should exist in the believer's relationship with God.

THE DANGERS OF SEX OUTSIDE OF MARRIAGE

1. Unwanted Children

People who selfishly engage in sexual activities outside of God's will often bring unwanted children into this world. Many of these children are born into unhealthy situations where they do not receive the attention of mature, loving parents who can meet their physical and emotional needs. Teenage pregnancies are often difficult on both the teen and the child. Furthermore, the majority of abortions occur as a result of unbiblical sexual activities.

2. Sexually Transmitted Diseases

Statistics of people with a sexuality transmitted disease (STD) are startling. Most of these diseases are incurable. They can lie dormant for years. A person can carry a disease, be contagious, and not know it. Some of these STDs increase the risk of certain cancers; some are painful; all can be embarrassing. Besides abstinence, no method of birth control can prevent contracting an STD. If two virgins marry each other, their chances of having an STD are virtually zero. If you suspect that you have an STD, you should get proper medical advice on how to best treat your disease, as well as how to prevent spreading it to others.

3. Broken Hearts

Many young people who think that they are in love are really being misled by the powerful desires of lust. Because of the strong desire to engage in sex, some people will pressure their reluctant partner to have sex with promises of love and marriage someday. Many young girls have lost their virginity believing these deceitful promises, only to have their hearts broken.

Imagine loving someone so dearly that you want to give that person the very best that you could give. You want to look your best, act your best, and be the best you can be for this person. You begin to discuss marriage, and your partner tells you that she has saved herself for the person that she will marry someday. You regretfully must admit that you cannot offer her the same gift. The tears running down her face would bring you pain that is difficult to bear.

4. Destroyed Marriages

Statistics indicate that people who have sex with each other before marriage are more likely to get divorced after their marriage. Though experts are not sure why this is true, it is possible that those who are willing to break the rules before marriage will be more likely to break the rules after marriage. Perhaps unresolved guilt that is carried into the marriage grows into bigger problems down the road. Relationships based primarily on sex do not allow for a healthy friendship to develop during the dating relationship. Premarital sex, even if it is only with the person you later marry, can lead to marital problems later in life.

It should go without saying that the sin of adultery destroys countless marriages. Though some married couples find a way to make their marriage work after adultery, they will always have the scars and memories of the adulterous relationship. Sadly, adultery usually leads to separation and divorce.

5. Destruction of Your Own Soul

All sin will result in a disharmony with God; many sins will result in disharmony with other people; sexual sins will bring disharmony with God, other people, and yourself.

CONCLUSION

Biblical sexuality is simple: save yourself for your spouse and then be faithful to your spouse. If everyone in society would do this, there would be fewer diseases, abortions, broken hearts, broken marriages, and children born into undesirable situations. It would have a direct, positive effect on the cost of welfare, health care, and crime. Though sins of homosexuality are serious, because of the number of people involved in heterosexual sins, it can be argued that heterosexual sins are more devastating to society than homosexual sins. Though you cannot change society by yourself, you can help ensure a happy relationship with your spouse someday and your relationship with the Lord today by living according to biblical principles regarding sexuality.

DISCUSSION/APPLICATION:

1. Some liberal-minded people advocate an aggressive sex education agenda in the public schools, beginning in elementary school. Do you think that this will hurt people or help solve problems related to sexuality in our society? Why?
2. Why do you think so many young people are willing to risk getting sexually transmitted diseases, heartaches, and unwanted pregnancies in order to engage in sexual activity? May there be a deeper spiritual need that people are trying to fulfill in the wrong ways?

Chapter 16

PORNOGRAPHY

SEXUALITY IS NOT JUST ABOUT the act of sex. If a person is trying to remain morally pure, there are other considerations besides being committed to saving oneself for marriage. Cinema, music, and television all are saturated with references to sex. More often than not, sex is presented in a perverted, cheapened form. Young people go around with a twisted view of sex long before they are supposed to begin thinking about it at all. By the time they get to an age when marriage becomes a realistic option, many teens enter into marriage with a defiled conscience and unrealistic expectations. Many of these marriages are doomed before they begin.

One of the most devastating influences on society in the area of human sexuality is pornography. The word "pornography" is associated with the Greek word *porneia*, often translated "fornication" in the New Testament. "Fornication" is a broad term that includes such ideas as homosexuality, premarital sex, and prostitution. The modern term "pornography" relates to what we could call mental fornication.

Pornography is nothing new. There are records of it from ancient times. There are obscene paintings on the walls of the ancient city of Pompeii, which was destroyed in A.D. 79. The invention of the printing press gave rise to getting all types of literature, both good and bad, into the hands of millions of people. As printing became more efficient and technologically advanced, pornographic magazines became popular. Their legal distribution was limited to adults; however, these were often discovered and viewed by minors. Ted Bundy, known for raping and murdering dozens of young women, began his lustful rampage as a teenager viewing pornographic magazines. Though most people will never stoop to the level of Ted Bundy, pornography is dangerous for all who choose to engage in it. It is addictive. It is unrealistic. It plants seeds of destruction that spring up years later to destroy potentially happy marriages.

With the accessibility of pornography by way of the Internet and other technological toys, the problem is worse than ever. The temptation is greater than ever. Like any sin, there are doorways into this sin that seem relatively innocent. Here are a few doorways that every parent and young person would do well to shut out of their lives:

1. Music that has immoral content.
2. Literature that contains sexually explicit content. This includes certain teen magazines, some fitness magazines, certain novels, and material available on the Internet.
3. All Internet access that does not have a family filter. A good filter can make finding pornography on the Internet much more difficult and can make accidentally coming across it nearly impossible.
4. Movies with themes or scenes that are immoral. Most movies have a rating that will state what content in the movie led to the particular rating.

Besides avoiding these doorways to potential disaster, it is important to have positive influences as well. Here are a few suggestions for teens and young singles to protect themselves from trouble as they tread over a landscape dotted with land-mines ready to explode:

1. Plant a hedge of protection. Begin by removing the weeds. These include the previously mentioned items related to media as well as friends who pull you down.

2. Your hedge of protection must include positive influ-ences. It isn't just about removing the bad. You must replace the bad with good activities and friends.

3. Rather than attempting a life of isolationism, do what you can to help others. Your efforts will strengthen you and encourage others. Don't preach to others in a judg-mental spirit, but try planning healthy activities with your friends.

4. Do not neglect your spiritual walk. Galatians 5 teaches that if one walks in the spirit, he will not fulfill the lust of the flesh. According to the Bible, it is not trying harder to do right that will keep you pure, but abiding in the presence of God.

CONCLUSION

There are many opportunities for people to mess up mor-ally. Pornography is one of the most common and dangerous sexual sins. Because of its availability, people need to develop standards to live by. Your heart, mind, body, and future spouse are worth the effort it will take to protect yourself from moral dangers.

DISCUSSION/APPLICATION:

1. How can you avoid the wrong kind of friends without com-ing across as a snob or a "holier than thou" kind of person?

2. Besides the things listed in this chapter, what other things can people do to protect themselves from sexual immorality?

3. Proverbs 6:32 says, "He who commits adultery lacks sense; he who does it destroys himself." Rewrite this verse in your own words. What do you think the writer means by the phrase "destroys himself"?

Chapter 17

MARRIAGE AND DIVORCE

MARRIAGE IS BY FAR the most influential societal institution in the world. The biblical basis for marriage and divorce needs to be reviewed in light of the current trend of attacking traditional marriages as well as the extremely high divorce rate. Many couples do not know what marriage means from a biblical perspective. The institution of marriage has been removed from its covenantal context in the Bible and has become for many a relationship of convenience that can be ended for any reason. A biblical knowledge of marriage and divorce is important for every Christian who is married or may become married someday. A few purposes of marriage include:

1. *Completion.* The wife completes the husband and the husband completes the wife. Though some people have a special gift for singleness (1 Corinthians 7), and therefore remain celibate, most humans need a companion to complete them physically, mentally, and emotionally. Eve was created as a "helper" for her husband Adam (Gen. 2:18). The Hebrew word for "helper" is closer in meaning to the idea of equal partner rather than servant. Regardless of the meaning of the word, the point is that Adam needed Eve to complete him.[1]

---

[1]For a detailed explanation of this point see Stephen A. Grunlan, *Marriage and the Family: A Christian Perspective* (Grand Rapids, Mich.: Zondervan, 1984), 146.

2. *Covenant to each other.* Marriage is a covenant between the partners (Mal. 2:14) with a vow before God to keep it. Many Christians view the role of the wife as being a servant to her husband. If this is true, then it is also true that the husband should serve the wife (Eph. 5:21). Their bodies are for the purpose of pleasing each other (1 Cor. 7:3-4). This attitude should extend beyond the marriage bed. The husband should be willing to lay down his life for his wife. The wife should submit to the husband's God-ordained authority as unto the Lord and to the extent that he is leading consistently with God's ways. A wife who has a husband who loves her the way that Christ loved the church will have little problem serving him (Eph. 5:22–28).

3. *Proper context for children.* As we saw in chapter 15, children do better socially when raised in the context of a loving family. Children learn the roles of male and female. The more the husband and wife live out biblical principles in a marriage, the easier it will be for the children to learn these roles.

4. *Physical pleasure.* Paul wrote that it is "better to marry than to burn with passion" (1 Cor. 7:9). He was not implying that sex was a necessary evil. In the context of this verse, he was praising the virtues of being single for the Lord. However, those who have strong sexual desires should marry. Sex is a gift from God that helps to physically and emotionally tie a married couple together into a closer union. Sex is best when it is practiced within a marriage relationship (Prov. 5:18).

Marriage is a lifelong commitment. In reference to marriage, Jesus said, "What therefore God has joined together, let not man separate" (Matt. 19:6). Marriage lasts for a lifetime on earth. Death dissolves the marriage (Matt. 22:30). Marriage should also be understood as a monogamous relationship (1 Cor. 7:2).

DIVORCE

The Lord hates divorce (Mal. 2:16 mg.). Dating and engaged couples should go into marriage with the assumption that it will last until one of them dies. Marriage vows made before God should be respected and honored as a covenant relationship.

The major New Testament passages about divorce include Matthew 5, Matthew 19, and 1 Corinthians 7, all of which teach against divorce. However, the two Matthew passages mention a possible exception:

> It was also said, "Whoever divorces his wife, let him give her a certificate of divorce." But I say to you that everyone who divorces his wife, except on the ground of sexual immorality, makes her commit adultery, and whoever marries a divorced woman commits adultery (Matt. 5:31–32).

> And Pharisees came up to him and tested him by asking, "Is it lawful to divorce one's wife for any cause?" He answered, "Have you not read that he who created them from the beginning made them male and female, and said, 'Therefore a man shall leave his father and his mother and hold fast to his wife, and the two shall become one flesh'? So they are no longer two but one flesh. What therefore God has joined together, let not man separate." They said to him, "Why then did Moses command one to give a certificate of divorce and to send her away?" He said to them, "Because of your hardness of heart Moses allowed you to divorce your wives, but from the beginning it was not so. And I say to you: whoever divorces his wife, except for sexual immorality, and marries another, commits adultery" (Matt. 19:3–9).

There are some believers who take the position that divorce or remarriage after a divorce is always wrong. They emphasize Mark 10:1–9 and Luke 16:18, where Jesus never mentions an exception for divorce. They also look at the exception clauses in Matthew 5 and Matthew 19 as references to sex before marriage (fornication) while the couple was betrothed. In the Old Testament, betrothal was more binding than an engagement of today. A certificate of divorce was necessary to absolve the betrothal even before the consummation of the marriage.

Others allow for divorce as a result of marital unfaithfulness. They interpret Jesus' exception clause more broadly as the New International Version reflects with the reading, "except for marital unfaithfulness." The New King James Version and the English Standard Version read "sexual immorality." The actual Greek word, *porneia,* sometimes translated "fornication," has both a narrow and a broad meaning. The narrow meaning can mean premarital sex. The broad meaning extends to any illicit sexual relationship. In this case the innocent party is free to remarry, but the guilty party is not. The one who commits adultery is breaking the covenant, not the innocent spouse. It would still be honorable to follow the example of Hosea and forgive the unfaithful spouse. However, repeated offenses may necessitate physical separation and divorce to protect the children from witnessing a bad example, and the innocent spouse from emotional pain and possible exposure to disease.

Within the Mosaic system, divorce was allowed as a concession, though it was never God's desire for the nation of Israel (Deut. 24:1). In the Matthew passages, Jesus sheds light on this Old Testament concession and says that divorce was allowed only because of the hardness of people's hearts. It never was and never will be God's perfect will:

> [10]To the married I give this charge (not I, but the Lord): the wife should not separate from her husband [11](but if she does, she should remain unmarried or else be reconciled to her husband), and the husband should not divorce his wife.
>
> [12]To the rest I say (I, not the Lord) that if any brother has a wife who is an unbeliever, and she consents to live with him, he should not divorce her. [13]If any woman has a husband who is an unbeliever, and he consents to live with her, she should not divorce him. [14]For the unbelieving husband is made holy because of his wife, and the unbelieving wife is made holy

because of her husband. Otherwise your children would be unclean, but as it is, they are holy. [15]But if the unbelieving partner separates, let it be so. In such cases the brother or sister is not enslaved. God has called you to peace. . . .

[26]I think that in view of the present distress it is good for a person to remain as he is. [27]Are you bound to a wife? Do not seek to be free. Are you free from a wife? Do not seek a wife. [28]But if you do marry, you have not sinned, and if a betrothed woman marries, she has not sinned. Yet those who marry will have worldly troubles, and I would spare you that (1 Cor. 7:10–15, 26–28).

These verses teach several things that Jesus did not specifically address in the Gospels:

1. A wife should not divorce her husband, even if he is an unbeliever.
2. A husband should not divorce his wife, even if she is an unbeliever.
3. If the unbelieving spouse leaves, the one who is left is no longer bound and is innocent of any wrongdoing in the matter (v. 15).
4. Whatever state one is in, it is best to remain there: if divorced, remain single; if married, remain married. (This idea is developed in more detail in verses 16–25, which were not included above.)
5. If a deserted spouse remarries or if a virgin marries, it is not a sin. (In verse 27, the word "free" is in the passive voice in the original Greek [literally, the word is "loosed"], implying that the person was deserted and was not the one who initiated the divorce. The phrase in verse 28, "but if you do marry," is a reference to the situation in the previous verse of one who has been loosed from being bound in marriage. This last point is not clear to all believers. Some disagree that these verses teach that these individuals are no longer bound to their marriage vows and are free to remarry. Some believe it means that they are at peace because of the separation.)

CONCLUSION

Divorce is not God's will. It never was. These views regarding divorce do not exhaust the positions of Christians regarding this issue. For a more detailed summary of various views, refer to the recommended reading list at the end of this chapter. Some conservative believers hold to a position that divorce or remarriage after divorce should never be permitted. A more moderate view allows for forgiveness and remarriage, recognizing that divorce is not an unpardonable sin. It also allows for special circumstances in which there may be a higher moral principle involved that calls for exemption from one's normal commitment, just as the Mosaic law allowed for it in the case of premarital infidelity. However, this does not mean that every effort should not be made to restore a marriage. Marriage is a covenant before God. It should be respected as such. Divorce should not be a part of an engaged couple's vocabulary. This "binding" of a couple in marriage should not be thought of in the sense of slavery or imprisonment. Marriage is a structure that provides safety, trust, and protection for both people in the relationship. Young couples should pray long and hard to discern the will of God before they enter into this binding and beautiful relationship.

DISCUSSION/APPLICATION:

1. In what ways is divorce hard on the couple's children?
2. How should churches minister to those who have been through divorce?
3. What sort of counseling regarding divorce should a pastor give to a couple considering marriage?
4. Why do you think that God is so strict when it comes to the divorce issue? Isn't it a bit too much to say that a person who makes a mistake in their twenties cannot be forgiven and remarry later in life? Consider different scenarios in light of the various passages in this chapter.

RECOMMENDED READING

Geisler, Norman L. *Christian Ethics: Options and Issues.* Grand Rapids, Mich.: Baker, 1989.

Grunlan, Stephen A. *Marriage and the Family: A Christian Perspective.* Grand Rapids, Mich.: Zondervan, 1984.

House, H. Wayne, ed. *Divorce and Remarriage: Four Christian Views.* Downers Grove, Ill.: InterVarsity, 1990.

Chapter 18

ECOLOGICAL ISSUES

He prayeth well who loveth well
  Both man and bird and beast.
He prayeth best who loveth best
  All things both great and small;
For the dear God who loveth us,
He made and loveth all.[1]

These lines are from the famous poem *The Rime of the Ancient Mariner.* Would God agree that to love animals is related to one's spiritual condition, particularly one's ability to commune with God? Should Christians make an effort to take care of the natural world? Is it wrong to dump harmful waste into the sea or to throw bags of garbage over a hillside? Is it sinful to destroy species of animals? On the other hand, isn't it true that God is going to destroy the world with fire in the last days? Why does it matter how we take care of the world since God will clean it up again one day?

Few topics are more hotly debated than ecological issues such as global warming and the role of government regulations through such agencies as the Environmental Protection Agency. Many scientists believe strongly in the reality of global warming. They believe global warming is caused by increased

---

[1]Samuel Taylor Coleridge, *The Rime of the Ancient Mariner* (Lewisville, Tex.: School of Tomorrow, 1993), 68.

carbon dioxide levels in the atmosphere, which result from emissions from fossil fuels used in factories, cars, planes, and other human activities.

The Intergovernmental Panel on Climate Change (IPCC) has been studying this issue and is in the process of publishing a series of lengthy and technical reports. This committee has concluded that global warming is occurring and that the results could be devastating over the next one hundred years. If these scientists are correct, humans can expect dramatic changes in weather patterns as well as coastal flooding. The worst weather changes could cause more natural disasters such as famines, floods, and powerful storms. Warmer weather could increase the population of certain pests and disease-causing bacteria and viruses. The impact on human life would be enormous.

There are other scientists who do not agree with such grim forecasts. And even if they do agree that the earth is getting warmer, they believe that there are explanations other than human activity for this warming trend.

One thing is certain: the political debate regarding global warming is getting hotter. However, the study of ecology is much larger than the global warming issue. The way humans regard the planet and the impact humans have on the planet is an issue with profound moral implications. Moving away from the political firestorm brought on by ecological debates, this chapter will look at ecology from a biblical viewpoint and offer principles that help to formulate a balanced position.

PRINCIPLE 1: GOD CREATED THIS WORLD AND SAW THAT IT WAS GOOD (GENESIS 1–2).

The universe belongs to God. It is His Sistine Chapel. A man who is in awe of a majestic mountain vista is a man in awe of God's ability to create. When a woman is able to find peace by a stream or the sea, she is being ministered to by God. Nature is good because it is God's work.

The doctrine of the fall of man implies that there was a negative effect on the natural world (Rom. 8:18-22). However, an imperfect universe does not negate the fact that the universe is the product of God's mind and in an imperfect way reflects His mind and will. It reflects something of His personality. Art students can quickly identify a work with a known artist. Often, an artist's mood, worldview, and knowledge about a subject can be perceived from a painting. Something of the mind of a computer programmer is reflected in the software he designs. Likewise, something of the mind of God can be understood by a meditation on His marvelous works. All created beings, animals as well as humans, have value because God created them.

PRINCIPLE 2: THE NATURAL WORLD IS A REVELATION OF GOD (PSALM 139; ROM. 1:19-20).

In Romans 1:19-20 the apostle Paul states that the invisible attributes of God can clearly be seen through the physical world. This is in the context of an important passage about salvation. God has revealed Himself to every human being through nature. In this sense, every human has access to God. To the extent that one chooses to embrace, ignore, or destroy this revelation of God, one is indirectly accepting, ignoring, or rejecting God. This choice may very well determine whether that person will receive additional revelation. At the very least, if one rejects this revelation of God in nature, he sets a precedent for rejecting God that may continue throughout his lifetime.

"Nature is the reflection of God. God is everywhere manifest; he is in the light and the darkness, on the land and in the sea, in the height and in the deep (cf. Ps. 139:7–12). The observing eye can see evidences of God everywhere."[2] To destroy nature is to destroy an important testimony of God. Doing so contributes to a distorted view of God; it has the potential to hinder evangelism; it is irresponsible and irreverent.

Wendell Berry uses more poignant words: "Our destruction of nature is not just bad stewardship, or stupid economics, or a betrayal of family responsibility; it is the most horrid blasphemy. It is flinging God's gifts into His face, as if they were of no worth beyond that assigned to them by our destruction of them."[3] Of all people, Christians should have a respect for the natural world of which we are an integral part. Yet this is too rarely the case.

An irony can be found in man's tendency to label a cathedral sacred but to diminish the reality of God's presence in a forest or a field. A house of worship can be a sacred place to the extent that worshipers acknowledge the presence of God. The art of stained glass windows or paintings can be an interpretation of and tribute to God's work. They can serve as an aid to worshipers in their quest to glorify God. Yet every "sacred" work of man is just an imitation or an interpretation or an extension of God's original design.

PRINCIPLE 3: GOD GAVE HUMANS THE RESPONSIBILITY TO HAVE DOMINION OVER AND CARE FOR THE EARTH.

"The earth is the LORD'S and the fullness thereof" (Ps. 24:1). As the hymn writer put it, "This is my Father's world." The earth is His. Another principle in Scripture that conflicts with the lack of regard for how natural resources are used or enjoyed is related to stewardship. Humans are stewards of God's creation. This stewardship includes commands to populate the earth, to subdue and rule over it, and to take

---

[2]Norman L. Geisler, *Christian Ethics: Options and Issues* (Grand Rapids, Mich.: Baker, 1989), 303.
[3]Wendell Berry, "Christianity and the Survival of Creation," in *Sex, Economy, Freedom, and Community* (New York: Pantheon, 1993), 98.

care of it (Gen. 1:28; 2:15). God has entrusted a segment of His creation to human care.

The dominion mandate of Genesis 1:26, 28 should not be interpreted as destruction but as preservation. One of the purposes of the natural world is to provide for human needs. There is nothing wrong biblically with utilizing natural resources to provide for human needs if it is done in a responsible manner. Genesis 2:15 provides further instruction on how this mandate is to be carried out. God told Adam to "dress and keep" the garden in which he was placed. This set a precedent for future humans to take care of the natural world.

PRINCIPLE 4: GOD IS CONCERNED ABOUT ANIMAL LIFE.

Though God does not place animals on the same level as humans as far as their basic worth, they are considered worthy of His watchful care. For instance, the Mosaic law had regulations about the treatment of animals (Deut. 22:4, 6–7). The Ten Commandments provided for animals to have a day of rest (Ex. 20:10). Balaam was reprimanded for beating his donkey (Num. 22:32). Valuable lessons can be learned even from a simple ant (Prov. 6:6). Animals have intelligence (Isa. 1:3; Jer. 8:7). Proverbs 12:10 says that a righteous man has regard for the life of his animal. Jesus taught that God provides for the birds (Matt. 6:26) and is concerned when a sparrow falls to the ground (10:29). In Old Testament times, even the land was to have a Sabbath rest every seven years. During those years no agriculture was to be done; whatever the land produced could be eaten by people, livestock, or wild animals (Lev. 25:1–7).

One of the theological giants of the church, revered by Catholics and Protestants alike, was Thomas Aquinas. He wrote that "humans owe it to God and his goodness to be compassionate toward animals. We are called to love and preserve creatures to his honor. And we honor God by exercising our rational dominion over animals and by preserving creatures whose very being as well as usefulness to us proclaim God's wisdom."[4] He also wrote, "If a man practices a pitiful affection for animals, he is all the more disposed to take pity on his fellow men."[5]

PRINCIPLE 5: GOD IS CONCERNED ABOUT THE PHYSICAL HEALTH OF HUMANS.

Many of Jesus' miracles related to healing people of physical illnesses. Though sometimes an illness is part of God's plan, and we all have a future appointment with death (Heb. 9:27), we should live clean lives that do not contribute to poor health. An irresponsible attitude toward the natural world could contribute to one's poor health as a result of consuming carcinogens and other toxins through air, food, and water.

Mercury in fish, increases in various cancers, and famines may be directly related to the exploitation of the natural world. There may very well be an endangered plant or animal somewhere in this world that holds the key to fighting off a disease like AIDS or cancer. Perhaps a potential cure has already been destroyed.

PRINCIPLE 6: GOD HAS A PLAN IN PLACE TO RESTORE THIS EARTH.

Prophecies related to the kingdom age describe a planet in which the curse has been lifted. Animals will coexist with humans in a state of harmony (Isaiah 11). This is the way things seem to have been in the garden of Eden. The Bible describes the earth as something currently groaning in pain, waiting for its own redemption. The doctrine of salvation and redemption applies not only to saving the souls of lost human beings but also to bringing a restoration to the natural world.

Many Christians are convinced that the Bible teaches that

---

[4]Thomas Aquinas, *Summa Theologiae*, IIaIIae, xxv, 3.
[5]Ibid., IaIIae, ci, 6.

Jesus will return to earth before humanity destroys it. It is true that the Bible teaches that the earth will not be uninhabitable at the time of Christ's return. Yet, this in no way guarantees that the natural world could not be in such bad shape that human survival would be very difficult. In fact, a literal interpretation of some Bible passages indicates that there will be serious environmental threats to human life as we approach the end times.

In a parable about stewardship and waiting on the kingdom, Jesus said, "Engage in business until I come" (Luke 19:13). No prophecy of the Bible sets a date for the return of Christ (Matt. 24:36). Many believers were convinced at the turn of both the first and second millennia that Christ would return then. Now, more than halfway through the first decade of the twenty-first century, we are still waiting. In the meantime, we had better think about the possibility that we are going to be here for a while. We must live as if our children and at least several generations of grandchildren will need a planet with clean air, soil, and water.

Furthermore, the passages that speak of a future destruction or judgment of the earth imply that the destruction is for the purpose of ultimate restoration of all things, including a new earth. None of these passages imply an annihilation of all things natural, but rather a restoration of the natural order. Whatever the true level of the coming destruction, it would be fitting that God the Creator be the one to destroy, not man the steward.

PRINCIPLE 7: HUMANS SHOULD LIVE IN HARMONY WITH NATURE.

How humans regard creation may not be the final test of faith; however, it is likely a reflection of how humans regard God. Teenage boys who find entertainment in blowing up small animals with firecrackers or playing baseball with frogs have obvious immaturity issues. These same boys may find it entertaining to light a fire and watch a field or forest burn. Yet, to say that they are just boys being boys is naïve. This mentality reflects something missing or wrong in the soul of humanity.

Humans originally were designed to live in complete harmony with nature. After the fall, this harmony was damaged but not completely broken. On a more serious level, the fall brought disharmony between the Creator and the creation. This enmity or disharmony between God and humankind is the state in which every human is born. Humans will never be fully content or satisfied in their existence until they are brought back into harmony with God. The New Testament teaches that this can only occur as a result of entering into a right relationship with Jesus Christ.

Just as the spirit of a person needs the Spirit of God, so the body of a person needs the physical world. A less obvious though equally important truth is that the physical body needs God and the spirit needs the natural world.

In one sense, nature is like the canvas upon which God painted the great masterpiece of the human race. Without the canvas, the paint has nothing to which to cling. Humans live in nature. Humans eat, breath, and drink nature. It is absolutely necessary to our physical survival. A human is more important than a rock or a tree; however, without the rocks, trees, and the rest of nature, human survival as we know it would be impossible.

In another sense, nature is like the paint on the canvas. All of nature is part of God's masterpiece on the canvas of space and time. All of His creation has intrinsic value. It can be used respectfully and should always be used reverently.

It would do us all well to remember that this is God's planet and that humans are just stewards. We are pilgrims passing through; other humans will need the earth long after we are gone.

DISCUSSION/APPLICATION:

1. What changes could you make in your life to be more in conformity with biblical principles related to ecology?
2. How does the sanctity-of-life principle relate to the issue of ecology?
3. Why do you think that Christians usually take strong positions on issues such as abortion and euthanasia and sometimes seem indifferent to issues related to poverty or ecology? Keep in mind that the sanctity-of-life principle applies to all of these issues.
4. What could you as an individual do to live more responsibly and respectfully in this world? Consider a group project with your class, perhaps taking an afternoon or Saturday morning to clean up a street or your school's campus. Consider beginning a recycling program at your school.

RECOMMENDED READING

Geisler, Norman L. *Christian Ethics: Options and Issues.* Grand Rapids, Mich.: Baker, 1989.

Snuffer, Ryan P. "Living Green for God." *Question Reality,* www.questionreality.org. Accessed March 2, 2007.

Chapter 19

ETHICS AND POLITICS

SHOULD CHRISTIANS LEGISLATE MORALITY? This question was dealt with in detail in a book titled *Legislating Morality.*[1] Though some Christians believe that they should not be involved in politics, this is not a biblical idea. If there were ever a vivid example refuting this fallacy it is the life of William Wilberforce in overthrowing slavery in England, as portrayed in the film *Amazing Grace.* Christians in democratic nations like the United States have the privilege of influencing the policies of their government every time they go to vote. There are special interest groups that inform leaders in government of issues and attempt to influence them accordingly.

The command of Jesus from the Sermon on the Mount to be salt and light applies to having a positive moral impact on the world (Matt. 5:13–16). According to the coauthors of *Legislating Morality,* the civil law does help implement changed attitudes and behaviors.[2] They cite two examples of how laws that have changed in America have influenced public opinion. The first of these is slavery. They point out that slavery was such a divisive issue in the 1800s that people were willing to divide the nation and go to war over it. In some regions, the majority of

[1]Norman L. Geisler and Frank Turek, *Legislating Morality: Is It Wise? Is It Legal? Is It Possible?* (Minneapolis: Bethany, 1989).
[2]Ibid., 37.

people, even those who called themselves Christians, supported slavery. Though change was slow following the Civil War, the vast majority of Americans now strongly oppose slavery.

A more contemporary example is the abortion issue. The coauthors of *Legislating Morality* write, "For nearly the first two hundred years of our nation's history, abortion was outlawed in all cases unless the mother's life was in danger. . . . In 1973, the vast majority of Americans believed abortion was immoral."[3] Just over thirty years after *Roe v. Wade*, the country was evenly split, with some polls indicating that the majority of Americans believed that abortion laws should be protected. Laws influence public opinion and perceptions of right and wrong.

An important point that they make is that all laws are in some ways a legislation of morality. To have laws against speeding implies that human life and safety is important—that it would be wrong to drive recklessly and endanger the lives of other humans or oneself. To have laws against murder, rape, and theft is to assume that these activities are wrong. Anytime a society has laws permitting or banning an activity, it is making a moral statement.

The real question regarding legislating morality is not whether or not to legislate morality, but whose or what morality should be legislated. The secular humanists have devised a system based on human reason and opinion. The *Humanist Manifestos I and II*[4] communicate certain moral positions regarding human rights. These statements are not based on a religious writing such as the Bible or a belief in God.

The theist's position is based on an understanding of the moral law that is universally present throughout all cultures. C. S. Lewis lists a collection of moral teachings from ancient writings throughout the world in the appendix of his book *The Abolition of Man*.[5] The similarities of these moral teachings

---

[3]Ibid.
[4]Paul Kurtz, ed., *Humanist Manifestos I and II* (Buffalo, N.Y.: Prometheus, 1973).
[5]C. S. Lewis, *The Abolition of Man* (San Francisco: HarperSanFrancisco, 1974), 83–101. First published in 1944.

argue for a universal understanding and interpretation of basic human morality.

Biblical theism goes a step further and uses the Bible as God's revelation to man. Within the Bible are found more details about what God considers right and wrong. Many secular humanists are against using the Bible as a source to influence laws in society because of its religious nature. Yet, using a document like the Humanist Manifesto in this sense is not much different. When people produce a document that makes moral claims about how people should or should not live in a society, they are making philosophical statements that have no objective basis.

The Bible is not the only source of truth. Believers are free to use reason and seek truth from God's general revelation as well (Ps. 19:1; Rom. 1:19; 2:12–15). For all truth is God's truth. To be sure, people have a tendency to interpret the Bible through their own biases. In the past, people have tried to use the Bible to justify such things as polygamy and slavery. However, to the extent that the Bible is properly understood in its historical context, the moral principles contained in its writings can and should apply to society today.

CONCLUSION

There is no reason that a Christian should not vote or try in other ways to have a positive impact on society. However, Christians should be wary of being too closely aligned with a particular political party lest they be in danger of blindly accepting an entire political platform. There are moral concerns all across the political spectrum in the United States. There has been moral triumph as well as moral failure in both major political parties. The record, integrity, and moral positions of individuals should be considered before you give them your vote.

DISCUSSION/APPLICATION:

1. Most evangelical Christians would generally align themselves with the Republican Party, in part because of the

issues concerning abortion and homosexuality. Name other moral issues on which our government has legislated. Is this good?

2. What political issues are most important to you? What do you think would have been most important to Moses, if he had lived under a democratic style of government? What do you think would have been most important to Jesus, if He had lived under a democratic style of government?

Chapter 20

ABORTION

"ABORTION ON DEMAND was recognized by the U.S. Supreme Court [in 1973] in its decisions on *Doe v. Bolton* and *Roe v. Wade*. In these decisions, the Court argued that the woman's right to privacy prevails over the state's interest in regulating abortions. As a result of these two decisions, abortion for any reason became legal in all fifty states."[1] There have been several rulings since this time to give states more regulatory rights; however, a woman can still have an abortion in any state. Other areas of controversy that have been debated in the political arena in recent years include the alleged right of a minor to have an abortion without parental consent or a woman's right to have an abortion without her husband's consent.

One victory for the pro-life side was the ban on partial birth abortion signed into law by President George W. Bush in 2005. Congress had previously supported this ban on three occasions only to be vetoed by President Clinton in the 1990s. Many were opposed to this method of abortion because it was a late-term procedure that resulted in the killing of the baby while it was capable of living outside of the mother. In some cases, the pregnancy was full-term. The baby was put to death as it was passing through the birth canal. If the baby had been completely out of the birth canal, its death would have been considered murder.

For most people, the debate hinges on when the baby is rec-

---

[1] Norman L. Geisler, *Christian Ethics: Options and Issues* (Grand Rapids, Mich.: Baker, 1989), 136.

ognized as a human being. As depicted in Table 20.1, there are three basic views regarding abortion: those who view the unborn baby as fully human, those who view the unborn baby as potentially human, and those who view the baby as subhuman.

Table 20.1
Three Views on Abortion[2]

Status of the unborn	Fully human	Potentially human	Subhuman
Abortion	Never	Sometimes	Anytime
Basis	Sanctity of life	Emergence of life	Quality of life
Mother's rights vs. rights of the unborn	Life of the unborn over privacy of the mother	Combination of rights	Privacy of the mother over life of the unborn

THE UNBORN AS SUBHUMAN

Those who are pro-choice can justify the killing of unborn babies by holding to what they view as the "subhuman" status of the fetus. Though few Christians hold to this view, there are a few references from Scripture that some within the pro-choice camp have used. In Genesis 2:7 the Bible states that God made Adam of the dust of the ground. He did not become a living soul until God breathed into him the breath of life. Job 34:14–15 and Isaiah 57:16 also indicate that human life is connected with breath.

The example of Adam was unique, however. Some see a deeper idea within the word "breath" in Genesis 2:7 that includes the notion of "spirit." The Hebrew word can be translated as wind, breath, or spirit. To say that breath is what makes one human is a simplistic interpretation of these verses. A person with a punctured lung or someone in surgery who stops breathing does not cease to be human during this interval of time. The Bible states elsewhere that "the life of the flesh is in the blood" (Lev. 17:11; see also v. 14 and Gen. 9:4). The processes of the circulatory system begin working in the first

---

[2]Adapted from ibid., 135.

month of development within the womb. The Scriptural arguments for the subhuman status of the unborn baby are therefore weak at best.

Other arguments that support this view include the following:

1. *Self-consciousness.* Since an infant in the womb is not self-conscious, it is argued that it is not human. Yet, no one has been able to prove that an infant is self-conscious either. If this is the criterion, then there would be nothing wrong with killing infants (infanticide). A person in a coma or a person asleep is not self-conscious. Yet few would argue that a person is not human while in one of these states.

2. *Safety of mothers.* It has been alleged that thousands of mothers died from infections as a result of illegal abortions before it became a legal, sanitary procedure. The simple answer here is that what the women were doing before was illegal. A society should not give in to the idea that it should accommodate and regulate evil just because it is going to happen anyway. One might also point out the difference in the numbers of *mothers* who died (perhaps thousands) before *Roe v. Wade* and the number of *babies* who have died since then (tens of millions).

3. *Abuse and neglect.* Since many of the women who choose abortion would be bringing children into a world of abuse and neglect, they are better off choosing not to have a child. This ignores the option of adoption. There are thousands of families seeking to adopt children and offer them a home with love and security.

4. *Rape.* No woman should be forced to have a baby fathered by a rapist, say the pro-choice advocates. It is understandable that they would feel this way, but it is also true that no woman should ever be raped. Two wrongs do not make a right. The murder of a baby will not cancel out the rape that occurred. This is a rare occurrence, with fewer than 1 percent of abortions fitting into this category. Abortion should not be kept legal for all situations just because of a rare situation such as rape resulting in pregnancy. These mothers, too, can choose adoption.

5. *Physical dependence.* Some argue that the baby is an extension of the mother; therefore, the mother has the right to exterminate this unwanted part of her reproductive system. Though it can be said that the baby is physically dependent on the mother during this time, it can be proven biologically that the baby is not just an extension of the mother. For instance, the genetic makeup of the baby is a unique combination of genes derived from the mother and the father. In many cases, the baby will have a different blood type from the mother. The unborn child is a unique person with a distinct biological identity and fingerprint.

6. *Privacy.* One of the major arguments in favor of abortion relates to the woman's right to privacy. It is believed that the Constitution guarantees the right of the woman over her own body. The same arguments we used against the physical dependence argument apply here. Though the Constitution may guarantee the right of an individual over her body, the baby is a separate person with a separate body.

THE UNBORN AS POTENTIALLY HUMAN

Those who see developing embryos as in a state of becoming human can justify early-stage abortions on the basis that the life-form is not yet human. This was the case in the ruling of *Roe v. Wade,* although it did not specify at which point the individual becomes a human. The DNA is present at conception. The heartbeat begins at eighteen days. All the body parts are present and functioning by the end of the second month. The baby reaches a point at which it can survive outside the mother's womb during the fifth month. Self-consciousness occurs sometime after birth. No one has been able to clearly define the exact time at which an embryo becomes human. It is a subjective dance of rational arguments with no clear defining line.

Part of the problem with this view is that human development is confused with the human essence. No one would argue that personality and body parts develop gradually over time, even throughout puberty and beyond. Yet, from a biological standpoint, the distinguishing characteristics of a human being are all present at conception in the form of DNA. Human social and spiritual characteristics will develop over time as a child grows up in a particular environment. However, a lack of physical, social, or spiritual maturity has nothing to do with whether a person is human. Personality is not equal to personhood. Possessing a spirit is not equal to spiritual growth. Nothing in science can either prove or disprove whether a person has a nonphysical, spiritual nature. If a person has a spirit, nothing in the scientific world can prove at what point the spirit becomes a part of the person. One must look in the arena of religion and faith to find answers to this sort of question.

THE UNBORN AS FULLY HUMAN

"Life begins at conception" is the belief of most of those who consider themselves pro-life. From a biological perspective, this cannot be denied; however, a more important issue is whether *human* life begins at conception or at some later point. If the spirit of a human is present or begins at conception, then it can be said that one is human at this point. There is no verse in Scripture that clearly defines the point in embryonic development at which human life begins. There seems to be the assumption that there is no point at which a developing embryo becomes human, but that it is human from the very beginning. Here are a few references from the Bible that support this point:

1. Unborn babies are called "children," the same word used for infants and young children (Ex. 21:22; Luke 1:41, 44; 2:12, 16).
2. God creates the unborn (Ps. 139:13) just as God created Adam and Eve in His image (Gen. 1:27).

3. The life of the unborn is protected by the same punishment for injury or death (Ex. 21:22–25) as for the injury or death of an adult (Gen. 9:6).
4. Personal pronouns are used to describe unborn children (Jer. 1:5; Matt. 1:20–21).
5. God intimately and personally knows the unborn just as He knows any other person (Ps. 139:15–16; Jer. 1:5).
6. God calls the unborn before birth (Gen. 25:22–23; Judg. 13:2–7; Isa. 49:1; Gal. 1:15).[3]

Outside of the Bible, scientists have taken both sides of the issue. The media often portrays these types of debates as science versus faith. However, there is a mixture of faith and science on each side. The real debate is motivated by a clash of worldviews. One side sees man as the measure of all things and the quality of life as more important than the sanctity of life. The other view believes in a morality rooted in the nature of the theistic God.

Because modern science has given us a window into the womb, it is possible that a problem with the baby could be detected that may give people a reason to consider abortion. Many parents who find out that their child is going to have some type of deformity or mental impairment choose to abort their baby. There is no biblical justification for abortion on these grounds. However, an exception that many people within the pro-life camp take is when the lives of the mother and baby are clearly in danger. For example, a tubal pregnancy will result in the death of both the baby and the mother if nothing is done. The baby will die whether the procedure takes place or not. A procedure in this case would actually save the life of the mother. The sanctity-of-life principle should give clear guidance in these life-and-death decisions.

If we truly believe that the unborn are fully human, then we should treat them as we would any other of our fellow humans:

---

[3]Adapted from ibid., 148.

Discriminating against anyone's life based on circumstantial matters such as size, age, location, or functional ability is morally wrong. Yet these are the same grounds on which abortionists consider the unborn child to be nonhuman. On these grounds we could discriminate against the lives of pygmies or preemies because they are too small, or against minorities because of where they live. Why then discriminate against babies who still live in the womb? Or we could discriminate against the handicapped or elderly because they lack certain functional abilities. And if we eliminate babies from the human community because they are unwanted, then why not discard other undesired segments of society, such as AIDS victims, drug addicts, or derelicts?[4]

CONCLUSION

If we think in terms of human DNA, it is a scientific fact that human life begins at conception. The biblical evidence points to the same moment. If human life begins at conception, then abortion is murder at any point during the pregnancy. If human life begins later, then that point must be defined. Abortions after that defined point would be considered murder. Because of political implications and an overall lack of objectivity, it is unlikely that this debate will go away anytime soon.

DISCUSSION/APPLICATION:

1. Wouldn't a baby be better off not being born than being born into a home in which it will be abused? In your discussion, consider that God is sovereign over life.
2. Many will remember the Scott Peterson double murder trial. Peterson killed his wife and unborn baby. Consider the inconsistency of the federal government's allowing abortion in any state, for any reason, and the fact that a person can be tried for murder for killing a baby while it is still in the womb.

---

[4]Ibid., 152.

3. Many politicians will imply that they are personally against abortion but that the mother, not politicians, should have the right to make the final choice. Is this a valid point or just political jargon?

4. What does the increasing indifference to human life say about the state of the human moral condition?

Chapter 21

EUTHANASIA

ON JANUARY 17, 2006, THE U.S. Supreme Court rejected the federal government's attempt to block Oregon's physician assisted suicide law. At the time of the writing of this text, Oregon was the only state that had legislation allowing for physician assisted suicides, though other states were discussing it. These suicides are allowed when a doctor has stated that a patient has only six months or less to live. Over two hundred people had received a lethal injection in Oregon between 1998 and 2005.[1]

Some fear that this ruling will set a precedent for cases likely to come up in other states. Others fear that once mercy killing becomes a widespread practice, the government will feel justified in ending the lives of patients in government facilities whom it considers not to have a "good quality of life." One California lawyer stated, "Once self-killing is an acceptable answer, how do you logically limit it to the dying? What about the disabled, who may live longer and suffer more?"[2]

The case of Terry Schiavo in 2005 helped many become more aware of the ethical debate associated with euthanasia. Terry Schiavo had been kept alive for years on life support. Her parents fought to keep her alive, but the government supported her husband, who stated that Terry would not have wanted to

---

[1] Cathy Lynn Grossman and Bill Nichols, "Some Hope for More Laws; Others Fear Them," *USA Today,* January 18, 2006, 5A.
[2] Ibid.

go on in her persistent vegetative state. Terry died on March 31, 2005, thirteen days after she was taken off life support.

With euthanasia, the issue is not as simple as asking whether it is right or wrong, since there are different types of euthanasia. These types are summarized in Table 21.1.

Table 21.1
Three Types of Euthanasia

Active Euthanasia	Unnatural Passive Euthanasia	Natural Passive Euthanasia
Taking a human life to avoid suffering	Deliberating withholding natural means to keep someone alive (food, water, air)	Withholding unnatural means to keep someone alive (kidney dialysis, respirator, organ transplants)

"Euthanasia," also called mercy killing, means "happy death." There are those who believe that the constitutional right to privacy includes the right to die with dignity. Proponents say that rather than suffer with a terminal illness or severe depression, an assisted suicide or self-inflicted suicide will bring dignity to the end of one's life.

ACTIVE EUTHANASIA

Active euthanasia is the form of euthanasia being discussed in courtrooms and legislative sessions across the United States today. Many churches and evangelical leaders have taken a strong stand against active euthanasia. Should humans be allowed to choose when their lives are terminated?

Besides believing that humans have a constitutional right to die with dignity, proponents have several ethical reasons to support euthanasia. They believe that euthanasia is an act of mercy to the sufferer. It reduces the amount of time a patient must suffer. It relieves the family and society of a great economic burden. It is a humane thing to do. Just as it is considered humane to euthanize a dog suffering from a terminal illness, so should we consider it humane to relieve a person from suffering.

RESPONSE TO ACTIVE EUTHANASIA

Critics of euthanasia point out that man has no moral right to intentionally kill another innocent human being. It is a form of homicide, whether it is by the hands of a physician or by one's self. Active euthanasia is in conflict with the sanctity-of-life and the sovereignty-of-God principles. It assumes that man has the moral right to decide when a person's life should end.

Sometimes God uses suffering to teach the one suffering or those around important lessons. Many of those who care for the terminally ill testify to being stronger, more spiritual persons as a result of their experiences. The argument of economic burden to the family and society is easily answered if one believes in the sanctity of life. No price tag can be put on the life of a person.

The right-to-privacy idea that some find in the Constitution is debatable; however, the right to life principle is clear from the Fifth and Fourteenth Amendments. Likewise, the Declaration of Independence speaks of certain "unalienable rights" endowed by the Creator that humans have. An appeal to the founding documents of this nation argues against euthanasia rather than for it.

The illustration about putting a dog to sleep is weak because a human is not just an animal. This is an argument influenced by a humanistic worldview, which says that man evolved from animals and was not created in the image of God.

UNNATURAL PASSIVE EUTHANASIA

Passive euthanasia can be divided into two categories—unnatural and natural. Unnatural passive euthanasia occurs when essential needs, such as food, air, or water, are withheld from the individual. To intentionally withhold any of these is the equivalent of murder. All of the arguments against active euthanasia apply here as well. When many people speak of euthanasia, they are speaking of either active or unnatural passive euthanasia. The third category, natural passive euthanasia, is not always referred to as euthanasia; however, because it also results in the death of a person as a result of withholding means that could keep the person alive, it can be referred to as a kind of euthanasia.

It is important to point out that few critics of euthanasia would be opposed to giving patients narcotics or other means to keep a person as comfortable as possible during their illness. The Bible states in Proverbs 31:6–7, "Give strong drink to the one who is perishing, and wine to those in bitter distress; let them drink and forget their poverty and remember their misery no more."

NATURAL PASSIVE EUTHANASIA

Natural passive euthanasia is withholding mechanical or other unnatural means from someone in order to hasten death. If this is in the case of a terminally ill patient, many Christians do not consider this wrong. These patients include people in a coma on life support or someone who is conscious yet kept alive by machines. There is no clear principle found in Scripture that would conflict with this idea. It is not *taking* life; it is simply *allowing* death to occur naturally. A man who is being kept alive only by artificial means should not be forced to use technology to keep himself alive. He can legally plan for this ahead of time in a living will in case he would reach a state in which he would not be able to make a decision for himself. This will prevent his family from having the burden of making this decision.

Dying is a process. Death is the culmination of that process. Once a terminal illness takes over the body, and unless God miraculously intervenes, it is just a matter of time before death occurs. If a person is suffering and dying, using artificial means to keep him or her alive can be viewed as prolonging death.

Critics of this view might suggest that, since life has intrinsic value, we should do everything we can in our power to keep humans alive. However, this could also be viewed as not trusting God's sovereignty enough to leave the matter in His hands. God can keep a person alive if He so chooses. He can work a miracle with or without the help of technology and medicine.

CLARIFICATION

One possibility of confusion is in the definition of the terms we are using. An expanded definition of unnatural passive euthanasia is "withholding natural means in their natural form from someone who needs these things to survive." In other words, even though air is a natural need, a respirator is not. To suffocate someone to death (i.e., not allowing them to get air naturally) is unnatural. To unplug a respirator is natural. To stop giving food to someone who is capable of eating is unnatural. To withdraw a feeding tube is natural in that it allows death to occur naturally.

Another point of clarification is that just because one might allow for natural passive euthanasia in some cases, one would not necessarily be comfortable with it in every case. A feeding tube and respirator are necessities during certain surgeries or because of certain illnesses, but the intention is to remove them when the person is capable of eating and breathing on her own. This is much different than the case of a person who is dying. Also, a person who is conscious, or could potentially regain consciousness, should be able to make this decision on his or her own.

There are also people who need a feeding tube for most or all of their lives but who otherwise can live a happy, normal life. There is no reason not to make efforts to keep such individuals alive.

CONCLUSION

Active and unnatural passive euthanasia should be rejected by the Christian on the basis that they are both forms of homicide and because they are inconsistent with the sanctity-of-life and sovereignty-of God-principles. Natural passive euthanasia is not inconsistent with any clear biblical principle and can be viewed as faith in God's sovereignty. Using artificial means of life support can be viewed as actually prolonging death. Each case should be considered in light of the circumstances and what seems to be the most loving thing to do for all those involved.

DISCUSSION/APPLICATION:

1. How does one's worldview influence which categories of euthanasia a person would consider ethically acceptable?
2. List the pros and cons of keeping one of your parents alive, should there be an unfortunate illness or accident resulting in the need for life support for an extended time with little hope of resuscitation.
3. Do you believe that the government should keep active euthanasia illegal, as it is in most states?
4. The Terri Schiavo case in Florida gained immense media attention, in part because of her failure to have a living will prepared so that her loved ones would not have to make the decision about whether to "pull the plug." Her parents wanted to keep her alive. Her husband wanted to pull the plug. Who do you think should have the right to make this life-and-death decision in this type of case?

Chapter 22

CLONING

"By which time the original egg was in a fair way to becoming anything from eight to ninety-six embryos—a prodigious improvement, you will agree, on nature. Identical twins—but not in piddling twos and threes as in the old viviparous days, when an egg would sometimes accidentally divide; actually by dozens, by scores at a time."[1]

This quote is not from a modern science lab room, but from Aldous Huxley's *Brave New World,* first published in 1932. *Brave New World* brought the concept of human cloning to the popular arena within the context of a science fiction novel. In Huxley's imagined world, sexual reproduction has become a thing of the past. Clones are mass-produced and manipulated to serve in different sectors of society.

The issue of cloning leapt from the pages of novels and became a part of public political debate in 1997 when Dolly the sheep was cloned. Human cloning refers to the cloning of actual human beings to produce human children or the cloning of human beings for biomedical research. A report of the President's Council on Bioethics stated,

For more than half a century, and at an accelerating pace, biomedical scientists have been gaining wondrous new knowledge of the workings of living beings, from small to great. Increasingly, they also are providing precise and sophisticated

---

[1]Aldous Huxley, *Brave New World* (New York: Harper Perennial, 1998), 7. First published in 1932.

knowledge of the workings of the human body and mind. Such knowledge of how things work often leads to new technological powers to control or alter these workings, powers ordinarily sought in order to treat human disease and relieve suffering.[2]

Many ethical dilemmas today are a direct result of advancements in technology. Scientists hope that human cloning can bring children to infertile couples. Perhaps a greater use of human cloning would be to aid in producing uniquely useful stem cells for studying genetic diseases and new therapies.

In 2001, American scientists produced the first human cloned embryos, but they died once they reached the six-cell stage of dividing.[3] Many nations, including the United States, banned human cloning in 2001. Yet the debate rages on. Many scientists believe that human cloning could eventually reduce human suffering by helping to find cures for diseases.

HUMAN CLONES

Asexual cloned reproduction can be achieved by placing the nuclear material of an existing human somatic cell (donor) into an oocyte (egg) whose own nucleus has been removed or inactivated. The fertilized egg is placed in the uterus of a female, who will give live birth to the baby clone. The result would be a human being genetically identical to the donor. They would be "identical twins," except that these twins may be years apart in age.

Children produced asexually by human cloning would not be born into traditional families. Emotional needs may be difficult to meet. Even if these children were put into foster homes, their identity would remain as clones of other humans. If these children were produced to give children to couples not able to have children, ethical concerns would include the many embryos that would likely die before a successful clone

---

[2]*Human Cloning and Human Dignity: The Report of the President's Council on Bioethics* (New York: Public Affairs, 2002), 5.
[3]Ibid., xxxix.

was produced. Some scientists advocate using human clones for research. The manipulation of human beings to serve the purposes of other human beings raises other serious concerns. The arguments in favor of human cloning as well as the moral problems of cloning humans are summarized as follows:

Purposes

1. Infertile couples could have genetically related children.
2. Cloning would provide an alternative for parents who are at risk of producing a genetically diseased child.
3. A child could be born who could be an ideal organ transplant donor.
4. A person could keep a connection with a dead or dying spouse or relative by having a clone produced of them.
5. Society could replicate individuals of great intelligence, talent, or beauty.[4]

Problems

1. All of the possible purposes of cloning focus on the benefits of parents and society at the possible expense of the clone. What about his or her well-being?
2. In experiments with animals, there is a 90 percent morbidity rate with attempts to initiate a clonal pregnancy. Furthermore, the live-born cloned animals suffer a high percentage of deformity and disability. If cloned humans growing inside the womb were observed to be deformed or disabled, the temptation would be to abort them. And what might be the fate of those born with deformities? It would be difficult to justify the killing of so many embryos and infants to produce one clone, whatever the purpose of the clone.
3. The idea of human beings manipulating life in this way is troubling to many. Some ethicists say that these scientists are playing God.
4. Cloned children may suffer emotional and psychological problems related to identity and individuality. These

---

[4]Ibid., xlvii.

children may be viewed not as gifts from God but as the products of man.

The conclusion of the report of the President's Council on Bioethics was that human cloning is unsafe and morally unacceptable. The sanctity-of-life and sovereignty-of-God principles would also imply that cloning to produce children is wrong.

CLONING FOR BIOMEDICAL RESEARCH

Should the cloning of human embryos be allowed for biomedical research? On the positive side, cloning for biomedical research can potentially lead to important knowledge about embryonic development and genetic studies that could lead to treatments and cures to diseases and disabilities. Stem cell lines could be developed and researched from special clones for advanced studies with great potential, according to advocates. On the negative side, many human embryos would have to be sacrificed in order to achieve any type of measurable success. Furthermore, there is no proof, only educated guesses, as to whether this area of medical research will produce any contribution to human health and happiness.

Some scientists believe that human embryos are not fully human and that using these embryos for scientific research in order to relieve human suffering is justified. Proponents say it should be understood that these embryos are not created for destruction but for the advancement of the quality of life. Most members of the President's Council on Bioethics agreed that the research should be limited to embryos up to fourteen days in development, before organ differentiation begins.[5]

---

[5]Ibid., lii.

OBJECTIONS TO CLONING FOR BIOMEDICAL RESEARCH

The council summarized some of the objections to cloning for biomedical research. These include:

1. The cloned embryo is genetically human and should be treated as an individual, not just as a mass of human tissue.
2. Though the purpose is not to destroy human life, the process of biomedical research on human clones will inevitably do so as embryos are destroyed. The end does not justify the means.
3. By crossing the boundary from sexual reproduction to asexual reproduction, the door is opened to genetic manipulation, research on later-stage embryos or fetuses, and "putting the federal government in the novel and unsavory position of mandating the destruction of nascent human life."[6]
4. The Christian would add to this list the reminder that life has intrinsic value and God is sovereign. Humans must respect and honor both of these principles. To try to escape death is futile. All humans suffer to some degree. To say that all suffering is bad is misleading. Much good can come out of suffering. Lessons of eternal significance may be learned by temporal suffering. Humans should attempt to help relieve suffering in the world; however, the destruction of some humans in order to help other humans cannot be justified morally.

CONCLUSION

Just because humans are able to do something does not make it right. Though the prospect of cloning to produce human children makes for interesting science fiction plots, it is inconsistent with important biblical principles. Cloning for biomedical research is also riddled with problems. Humans should respect

---

[6]Ibid., lvi.

the sanctity-of-life principle as well as moral limits related to life and death. It is good to improve the quality of life of humans by relieving suffering; however, it is too great a price when it is at the expense of other human beings.

DISCUSSION/APPLICATION:

1. Can you imagine a world in the future in which clones and normally conceived humans would coexist? What potential problems could arise with this new class of human beings?
2. What if another country that allows and funds research on human cloning and stem cell research comes up with successful cures or treatments of certain diseases? Wouldn't Americans have to admit that they were wrong to ban human cloning? Would we be justified in taking advantage of their new-found medical knowledge? Why or why not?
3. How does the sanctity-of-life principle relate to the issue of cloning?

Chapter 23

STEM CELL RESEARCH AND OTHER BIOMEDICAL ISSUES

STEM CELL RESEARCH

Human embryonic stem cells are the building blocks of life. The cells are unspecialized but are capable of differentiating into any cell in the human body. This occurs naturally early in pregnancy. Within a few weeks, these cells become the specialized tissues and organs that the human baby will be born with. Scientists are currently studying the mechanisms that cause those changes in the embryonic stem cells to occur. A single embryo can produce a family of constantly dividing stem cells that do not differentiate.[1] Scientists are hopeful that someday they will be able to grow tissues and organs to help those with serious diseases. At this point, it is mere speculation whether diseases like multiple sclerosis, juvenile diabetes, cancer, and Parkinson's disease will ever be successfully treated with the application of stem cell research.

One of the moral dilemmas in stem cell research relates to its use of aborted embryos and fetuses. In 2001, President George W. Bush allowed scientists access to federal funding to research existing stem cell lines. The move frustrated conservatives and liberals alike. Bush, who is against abortion, justified

---

[1]See Raymond S. Edge and John Randall Groves, *Ethics of Health Care: A Guide for Clinical Practice* (New York: Thomson Delmar Learning, 2006), 313.

the action based on the fact that the embryos had already been aborted. The evil had been done; perhaps some good could come out of the existing lines. Liberals thought the decision was too narrow. They believed that the federal government was being stingy and that potential cures to diseases would be delayed. Bush's decision did not limit how private funds could be used in stem cell research.

In July 2006 the Senate passed a bill allowing for expanded federal funding for stem cell research. When the bill reached the president's desk on July 19, he vetoed it.

One might ask, why not just continue to research using already aborted embryos from abortion clinics? Though the answer is not quite as simple as the question, doing so could create a market for aborted embryos and make it more difficult to pass legislation to reduce the number of abortions. Another point relates to the fact that the end does not justify the means. Though the end or goal is good (to cure diseases) this particular means to get there is not necessarily good.

Another point people sometimes make is related to the availability of stem cells from other sources such as umbilical cords and adult brain stems. There are no serious moral objections to stem cell research if the stem cells come from sources that do not relate to abortion in any way.

It must be kept in mind that stem cell research is a long way from fulfilling the hopes and dreams for curing many diseases. Sometimes the complexity of the issue is reduced to a slogan on a bumper sticker near election time. It is important for Christians to read about these issues so that they can make intelligent decisions and have intelligent discussions with other people.

AMNIOTIC FLUID–DERIVED STEM CELLS

A new promising area of study is known as amniotic fluid–derived stem cell research. Dr. Anthony Atala, director of the

Institute for Regenerative Medicine at Wake Forest University, has been doing research for several years with stem cell lines derived from the amniotic fluid of women during pregnancy. These stem cells offer many possibilities. Dr. Atala and his team have developed bone, muscle, neural, bladder, pancreatic, and liver tissues from stem cells derived from amniotic fluid. This area of research avoids the controversy of having to terminate developing human embryos. There is some criticism of this new area of research coming from proponents of embryonic stem cell research. Since these stem cells are about ten weeks more mature than embryonic stem cells, there are some limitations that embryonic stem cells do not have. However, Dr. Atala pointed out that amniotic fluid–derived stem cell lines are very close to embryonic stem cells. He also mentioned that amniotic fluid–derived stem cell lines seem less likely to produce tumors than embryonic stem cell lines.[2]

The implications of amniotic fluid–derived stem cell research are huge. It is possible that within the next couple of decades, many people could be receiving tissue and organ transplants derived from stem cells that do not require the destruction of human embryos. In fact, some humans have already benefited from another source of stem cells—those found in the tissue of human organs. Dr. Atala has successfully replaced, in several children, bladders grown from stem cells derived from the patients' own cells.[3]

GENETIC TESTING

Genetic testing has come a long way since the science fiction movies and comic books of the 1950s and 60s. The most common form of genetic testing today is designed to help expectant parents know if their child will have genetic impairments or deformities. Some parents choose to abort

---

[2]Anthony Atala, in discussion with Ryan P. Snuffer, April 26, 2007.
[3]http://www1.wfubmc.edu/news/NewsArticle.htm?Articleid=1821 (posted April 3, 2006).

their child once they find out this information. Other parents have no intention to abort their child. As a result of genetic testing, they are more informed and can better prepare to care for their child.

Persons can now be tested to see whether they are predisposed to certain diseases. The ramifications of this are varied. Positively, people can have a better idea of what lies ahead regarding their health. For instance, a person found to be genetically predisposed to a certain kind of cancer can learn about nutritional and environmental strategies that could help to prevent that cancer. Negatively, health insurance companies could label such people as too high-risk to be offered reasonable coverage.

One obvious moral problem is when couples choose to abort babies to avoid having a child not considered normal. Social problems also arise when people are labeled high-risk and as a result cannot get certain jobs or health insurance. If genetic testing ever becomes as commonplace as some envision, HIPAA regulators,[4] other government officials, and health care providers must make efforts to protect the privacy of the patient.

BIRTH CONTROL

There are three basic approaches to the birth control issue: it is never, sometimes, or always permissible. Of course, those who are not married should not need birth control since they should not be sexually active. However, it is important to be exposed to some of the issues related to birth control that readers may face now or in the future.

---

[4]In 1996, important legislation was passed known as the Health Insurance Portability and Accountability Act (HIPAA). This was enacted to provide patients better privacy and confidentiality. There are now civil and criminal penalties for health care providers who knowingly violate patient privacy. HIPAA guarantees patient rights regarding the ability to access health records or to amend them. Health care providers are now required to give patients clear written explanations about the patient's health conditions. Patients can control what and how much information can be shared with other health care providers. Some were opposed to the legislation because of the extra overhead costs for health care; it was ultimately passed on the grounds that it was ethically important to protect the privacy of the patient.

1. Those who believe that birth control is never permissible believe that birth control is a form of playing God. One of the purposes of sex is reproduction. Children are a blessing from the Lord. To take measures to prevent children from being born is unbiblical, according to many of those against birth control.

2. Those who believe birth control is sometimes permissible are usually divided on the issue of birth control pills and medications that may cause spontaneous abortions. Oral contraceptives ("the pill") have hormones that are meant to prevent pregnancy. In most cases this is what happens; however, if an egg is fertilized, the pill also acts to prevent the fertilized egg from being implanted in the uterus. Though more than 95 percent of the time pregnancy is prevented, the few spontaneous abortions caused are not worth the risk. Though many pregnancies naturally end up as miscarriages, taking medication to cause a miscarriage is immoral.

3. Christians who believe that birth control is always permissible for married couples will point out that God has given humans the ability to think and discover new ideas. Medical advancements have made life easier on a number of levels. Birth control is a means of family planning that couples have the right to utilize. Using birth control to prevent pregnancy is no more playing God than abstaining from sex to prevent pregnancy. Furthermore, there are moral problems with married couples abstaining from sex for extended periods of time (see 1 Cor. 7:1–5). Birth control allows more freedom within a marriage.

Some Christians say that the fear of causing spontaneous abortions using oral contraceptives is unwarranted. The Association of Pro-life Physicians states that using oral contraceptives drastically reduces the total number of spontaneous abortions in women. This figure is reached by pointing out that 20 percent to 30 percent of pregnancies in women not using any kind of contraceptive end up as spontaneous abortions.

By preventing pregnancy more than 95 percent of the time, the pill also greatly reduces the total number of spontaneous abortions.

DISCUSSION/APPLICATION:

1. Which of the views related to birth control do you believe is the best? Explain your answer.
2. Reflecting on previous chapters and other knowledge you have, list and/or discuss the pros and cons of the impact modern scientific knowledge has on ethical issues. List the ethical issues that would have been nonissues one hundred to two hundred years ago.
3. Cryonics is the study and practice of freezing human beings with terminal illnesses with the hope of resuscitating them in the future once a cure for the illness has been discovered. No one has successfully thawed a frozen human being. Some say that this will always be impossible. What are the potential ethical dilemmas related to cryonics?
4. Write a one-page summary of a biomedical issue not covered in this chapter (test-tube babies, surrogate motherhood, fertility drugs, forced vaccinations, etc.). One-third of the page should be a summary of the issue. The other two-thirds should describe ethical implications of this issue. These papers can be presented before others in your group or class.

Chapter 24

CAPITAL PUNISHMENT

CAPITAL PUNISHMENT IS putting someone to death for a crime that person committed. There are three basic views regarding capital punishment: rehabilitationism, reconstructionism, and retributionism.

REHABILITATIONISM

Proponents of rehabilitationism believe that there should never be capital punishment for any crimes. Christians and non-Christians alike hold to this view. It is based on the idea that the purpose of justice is rehabilitation and not retribution, hence the term "correctional facility" is to be favored over the term "prison." A correctional facility is a place to heal, receive counseling, and learn how to fit in with society. A prison is not a place of punishment.

Some secular humanists support this position because they do not believe in sin or evil as something real; therefore, people should not be punished for something that is not really their fault. People only do that which they are programmed to do genetically or environmentally. The internal and external factors affecting a person can sometimes influence him or her to do something that is not socially acceptable. Genetic or physiological problems can sometimes be corrected by medical procedures or drugs. Since environmental factors can sometimes influence behavior, one can often overcome or correct aberrant behavior by changing one's environment. Education, money, human relationships, and counseling can sometimes help someone heal.

Christians who are in favor of rehabilitationism often cite passages from the New Testament showing that Jesus promoted peace, tolerance, and forgiveness. For example, in the Old Testament, a women caught in adultery could be stoned to death; Jesus let such a woman go and told her to sin no more (John 8:1–11). Capital punishment was part of the Mosaic civil law, which was abolished along with the rest of Moses' law. The cross, according to this view, was the capital punishment for all people. Even in the Old Testament, exceptions were made, such as with Cain and with David. Ezekiel 18:23 asserts that God has no pleasure in the death of the wicked, but "rather that he should turn from his way and live." It seems here that God's desire is to cure the sinner, not kill him.

A few moral arguments against capital punishment include the following:

1. Capital punishment is sometimes unjustly applied. If there were even a small chance that some innocent people would be put to death, then a society should never take that chance.
2. Criminals should be cured not killed (Ezek. 18:23).
3. Capital punishment is inhumane.
4. If Christians believe in hell, why would they want to hasten a person's arrival there by putting him to death?
5. Christians should be quick to forgive. God is the judge. He will not acquit the wicked.

RECONSTRUCTIONISM

Proponents of reconstructionism view justice as retributive rather than rehabilitative. They also view the Old

Testament civil law as meant for all people at all times. Reconstructionists hold to capital punishment for all major crimes. This view has the least support among Christians, but it is worth mentioning since there are a few groups that would advocate applying its principles in society at large. There is even a small political party (at the time of the writing of this chapter) known as the Constitutional Party that holds to a view that Old Testament Law should be applied in modern society. There were over twenty offenses mentioned in the Old Testament that were punishable by death. These include murder (Ex. 21:12), rebellion by children against their parents (Ex. 21:15, 17), causing a miscarriage (Ex. 21:22–25), witchcraft (Ex. 22:18), idolatry (Ex. 22:20), false prophecy (Deut. 18:20), and rape (Deut. 22:25).[1]

Few people take seriously any attempt to reinstate Old Testament Law. Neither would have Jesus or the apostles. Those sins which were punishable by death in the Old Testament are still sins today because they are based on God's unchanging character; however, there is no reason to believe that God ever intended for every society to follow the theocratic model of ancient Israel, certainly not with all its capital crimes.

In addition to the example of Jesus and the adulterous woman, one could point out that the most severe punishment for any type of sexual sin mentioned in the rest of the New Testament was excommunication from a local church, not execution (1 Cor. 5:5).

Throughout the New Testament it is clear that the Old Testament Law was fulfilled in Christ. Romans 6:14 teaches that believers are "not under law but under grace." Later Paul writes, "Christ is the end of the law" for believers (Rom. 10:4). If one still accepts the Law of Moses as binding on people today, it is like rejecting what Christ accomplished on the cross (Gal. 3:21; see also 2 Corinthians 3 and Hebrews 8).

---

[1]For a more complete list read Exodus 21–22 and Leviticus 20–22. Also see Norman L. Geisler, *Christian Ethics: Options and Issues* (Grand Rapids, Mich.: Baker, 1989), 200.

RETRIBUTIONISM

Retributionism holds that capital punishment is legitimate for some major crimes, especially murder. Like reconstructionists, retributionists believe that the primary purpose of justice is to punish. However, retributionists do not believe that the Mosaic law is binding today. The Mosaic law does, however, set a precedent in that God did approve of capital punishment for certain specified crimes.

Even before the Mosaic law was established, Noah was given the authority to set up a government in which the shedding of human blood should be avenged (Gen. 9:5–6). Furthermore, the New Testament teaches that the government has the right to "bear the sword" and punish evildoers (Rom. 13:4). Since capital punishment was allowed before, during, and after the establishment of the Mosaic law, there is no reason to suggest that a government does not have the authority to execute criminals today, especially in the case of murder. Since there is no mention of governments having a God-given right to execute criminals for lesser offenses (outside of the Mosaic law), then one cannot use this logic to propose capital punishment for offenses other than murder.

Proponents of capital punishment for murder make several points:

1. It is based on a biblical view of justice without going to the legalistic extreme of reconstructionism.
2. It protects innocent lives by deterring crime and reducing the number of repeat offenders.
3. It is based on a high view of man that reveres the sanctity of the life of the victim, as well as potential victims. It also respects the dignity of the criminal as a rational, moral being; it does not reduce the criminal to the level of an animal completely controlled by genetic and environmental factors.
4. The Bible gives governments the right to execute crimi-

nals for capital offenses. Before the Law of Moses, God told Noah to form a system of government in which those who shed men's blood would have their blood shed by men (Gen. 9:6). After the Law of Moses had been abolished in the New Testament, Paul wrote that the government had the right to use the sword in order to punish evildoers and protect its citizens (Rom. 13:1–4).

RESPONSES FROM A REHABILITATIONIST PERSPECTIVE

1. Capital punishment does prevent all repeat crimes by that person. Beyond this, there is no clear statistical evidence that capital punishment deters crime. Some nations, such as Canada, have experienced a decrease in the murder rate since abolishing capital punishment. In the United States, the murder rate went up in the 1960s and 1970s when capital punishment was not widely practiced. But it is also true that nonviolent crimes increased during these decades. Perhaps there were other factors that skewed the statistics that make it difficult to draw a clear conclusion. It is also counterproductive to compare states with the death penalty to states without the death penalty since there are many demographic and cultural differences from state to state that can account for murder rates.

2. A truly biblical view of man will not only acknowledge a person's moral responsibility but will also acknowledge the sinful fall that has plagued mankind since the time of Adam. A high view of man must be balanced with compassion for the criminal's soul and family. Retributionism takes the "eye for an eye" mentality to the extreme and leaves little room for ministering to the sinner.

3. The *right* to execute criminals does not mean that the government is *required* to execute criminals. Governments have the responsibility to protect their innocent civilians. If a system can be proven to protect its citizens as well as rehabilitate criminals, it should be considered.

CONCLUSION

Since love is the absolute by which all ethical approaches should be measured, it must be mentioned in reference to capital punishment. Even within a system of retributionism, no Christian should take pleasure in the death of a criminal. The Bible certainly allows for a government to execute criminals who have committed murder. Some would say that it is not just the government's right but also its duty in order to protect its citizens and justly punish the criminal. Others, motivated by compassion, are looking for better ways to handle those who commit violent crimes.

DISCUSSION/APPLICATION:

1. Many other passages in the New Testament support the point that believers are no longer under the Law of Moses but under grace in Jesus Christ. Look up the following passages and discuss how these passages can be used to refute reconstructionism (Gal. 3:24–25; Hebrews 7–8).
2. Do you think that capital punishment saves lives in the long run? Should the issue of saving lives be at the center of this debate?
3. Though it can be proven from Scripture that a government has the right to execute murderers, does a right necessitate action? In other words, if a government could find an alternative system that works just as well as one that uses capital punishment, would it also have the right to establish that system? What kind of a system do you think might work just as well as capital punishment? Your system would have to result in fewer murders taking place in a given time period.
4. Research statistics on the Internet to see if capital punishment deters crime. Proponents will say that it does. (However, they may also say it would work better if criminals could be executed in a timelier manner instead of sitting through a lengthy appeals process.)

5. If you took the position of retributionism, how would you answer a critic who quotes Jesus saying to turn the other cheek and to love your enemies?

6. If you took the position of rehabilitationism, how would you answer a critic who reasons that a murderer has lost his right to live since he has taken the life of an innocent person?

Chapter 25

WAR

JESUS SAID THAT toward the end of the present age there would be "wars and rumors of wars" (Matt. 24:6). Never has this seemed more applicable than in the twentieth and twenty-first centuries. No century witnessed more bloodshed than the twentieth. However, to say that war is something new would be far from the truth. Every century has witnessed war on some part of the globe. The biblical record of the history of conflicts in the ancient Middle East demonstrates that even God's chosen people often went to war.

Christians take three main views regarding war. Pacifism is an approach that will avoid killing in war at all costs. Pacifists believe that war is always wrong. Activism views all wars as justifiable. If a nation declares war on another nation, citizens of that nation are obligated to support the war. Selectivism is an approach that views some wars as justifiable and others as unjust, depending on the circumstances. Many books have been written on these three approaches to war. The major points of each view are summarized in this chapter.

PACIFISM

Arguments for Pacifism:

1. The biblical command to not kill (Ex. 20:13) reveals something about the heart of God. War always results in killing, including the killing of innocent civilians.

2. Jesus taught a message of peace, including to love your enemies (Matt. 5:44) and to not resist one who is evil, but turn the other cheek (Matt. 5:39).

3. Since humans are made in God's image, people should never kill other people.

4. War does not solve problems; it only creates more problems. The conflicts in the Middle East illustrate this point. Killing inspires acts of vengeance. The cycle stops only after many people on both sides have been killed.

5. Using violence to stop violence is hypocritical. It sets a bad precedent for others to follow. Romans 12:19–21 teaches that we should overcome evil with good.

6. War seems to provoke retaliation and hatred. The First World War was naïvely advertised as the war to end all wars. History has proven otherwise. World War II was even more deadly than the First. The current War on Terrorism is proving that the twenty-first century will not be one of peace.

7. One is under the moral command to promote peace and resist evil with good whether wearing a military uniform or not. The distinction between the person and the office is unbiblical and inconsistent.

Arguments against Pacifism:

1. The command from Exodus 20 relates to murder, not to just any type of killing. It is clearly wrong to murder; however, within the Mosaic system, capital punishment was allowed for many reasons. Furthermore, there were times when God commanded His people to go to war.

2. Pacifism is unrealistic. If a nation is not prepared to go to war for self-defense, any other aggressive nation could take over. Other groups or nations could use violence against a nation trying to live the pacifist ideal.

3. A government that is not willing to go to war is a government not able to protect its people, which is clearly one of the responsibilities of government. What should nations have done, for instance, when Hitler was trying to take over the world?

ACTIVISM

Arguments for Activism:

1. God ordained government. God gave the government, first through Noah, the right to take the life of those who commit murder (Gen. 9:6). Though the form of government changed throughout the Old Testament, God's continued approval of government is observed through the Mosaic theocracy, the times of the judges, and the kings. There were many times when God directly commanded His people to go to war by communicating to specific leaders whom the people were to follow.

2. Romans 13 teaches that there is no authority except of God, and that whoever resists such authority is resisting the ordinance of God. Since God ordains governments, man has no right to resist their authority.

3. God sometimes uses an evil government to accomplish His purpose. God used evil pagan nations to judge Israel on multiple occasions. In the context of the Babylonian captivity, Daniel said to a pagan king that "the Most High God rules the kingdom of mankind and sets over it whom he will" (Dan. 5:21).

4. One does not have to agree with a government in order to obey it. God will hold those in leadership responsible for their decisions, not those under their authority.

5. There is the option of a person leaving his government by immigrating to another country. Socrates permitted this as long as the governed was not leaving in the face of duty; the person would have to leave before being called upon to go to war or service.

6. Some would reason that since disobeying government leads to revolution and anarchy, it is better to support your nation in a time of war, even if your nation is evil. The argument is that the evil of obeying an evil government is greater than the evil of chaos and anarchy. One can believe that somehow justice will triumph in the end.[1]

[1]Norman L. Geisler, *Christian Ethics: Options and Issues* (Grand Rapids, Mich.: Baker, 1989), 221.

Arguments against Activism:

1. Just because God ordains government does not mean that everything that a government does should be supported. God certainly does not ordain evil, though He sometimes allows it.
2. There are examples in the Bible of believers not submitting to the authority of the government. A dictator committing genocide should be resisted by his own citizens as well as by other nations.
3. Jesus consistently taught a message promoting peace and love toward enemies. Certainly peaceful resolutions should be preferred and sought for by the citizens of a nation, even when the leadership wants to fight a war.

SELECTIVISM (JUST WAR)

Arguments for Selectivism:

1. Selectivists do not believe in going to war for just any reason, but are realistic in acknowledging that war is sometimes necessary.
2. In opposition to activism, the Bible teaches that one is not required to obey the government when it contradicts the higher moral laws of God. The Hebrew midwives, Daniel, and the apostles all disobeyed their governments when those governments were in conflict with God's higher moral laws.
3. In opposition to pacifism, the Bible does not view military service as an evil occupation, but a ministry of God to execute justice as an extension of the government (Rom. 13:4).
4. Nations have a right to defend themselves. Governments have a responsibility to protect their people.
5. Many selectivists adhere to the widely accepted "just war theory," which can be summarized by the following points:[2]
   a. Defense of the innocent or self-defense against an

---

[2]Several of these points have been adapted from Geisler, *Christian Ethics,* 233–234. Quotation marks denote direct quotations.

aggressor is just. Sometimes the just nation must invade in order to establish peace, if the aggressor has invaded first; however, "the invaded country does not have the right to permanently occupy the invading country."

b. Wars fought to execute justice are just. The example of the Allied nations against Hitler is a good case in point. Hitler's Germany needed to be punished. Retribution is justified; however, once a nation surrenders, the focus should be on war criminals and leaders, not retaliation against the entire nation. Preemptive strikes are not justified unless there is intelligence that "a devastating first strike is imminent." Even then, the preemptive strike should not devastate the potential aggressor.

c. A just war must be fought justly. Innocent civilians should never be targeted. Weapons should be appropriately used. The ecological impact should be considered for those who will need to live there after the war is over.

d. Only a government has the right to wage a war. Private citizens and private militias are not justified in waging wars.

e. Peaceful options should be exhausted first. Peace, not conquest, should always be the goal of a just war.

f. A war should be fought only if there is a reasonable hope for success. Fighting a war that cannot be won cannot be justified. Many people will die needlessly.

People who claim to be selectivists sometimes have a blind loyalty to their nation that results in supporting any war their nation wages. The selectivist who is living consistently with God's ideal will have the heart of a pacifist and the wisdom to understand that there are times when, in order to protect and promote peace, force is necessary. It would do all believers well to remember that Jesus is referred to as the Prince of Peace—that He promoted the idea of peace while on earth and has promised to bring peace to this world someday. At the time of His return, He will truly lead the war to end all wars (Rev. 19:11–16; 21:4).

CONCLUSION

The Bible can be used to support any one of these positions when using only selected proof texts. However, taking the entire Bible into consideration, especially the teachings of Christ, it seems that the most biblical approach is selectivism but to go to war only when all other means to peace have been exhausted. Just as a husband is responsible for protecting his wife and children, so a government is responsible for protecting its citizens. There are times when a nation may need to wage war if it is going to responsibly protect its citizens. However, those in leadership roles in government should not take their responsibilities in making such decisions lightly. These decisions will undoubtedly impact the preservation or loss of many lives. Perhaps Americans could learn from certain nations that have managed to avoid conflicts over the years while at the same time preserving the peace of their citizens.

DISCUSSION/APPLICATION:

1. Do you think that the War on Terrorism is an example of a just war? More specifically, do you think the war in Iraq that began in 2003 is a just war? Why or why not?
2. Which approach to war from this chapter do you think is the most biblical? List reasons from this text. Feel free to add other reasons from the Bible or other sources.
3. How should believers reconcile the words of Jesus to love enemies and turn the other cheek with the commands of God in the Old Testament for Israel to go to war against Canaan?

Chapter 26

SUBSTANCE ABUSE

THE PRACTICE OF ALCOHOL and drug abuse is thousands of years old. The earliest Scripture reference to drunkenness involved Noah, just after he had brought his family through the flood (Gen. 9:21). The Bible repeatedly warns of the dangers of strong drink or of drinking alcohol in excess (Prov. 23:29–35; Rom. 13:13). There are several reasons that drunkenness is a sin:

1. Too much alcohol impairs one's judgment. Many moral mistakes have been made by intoxicated people. Some people become violent when intoxicated. Today, thousands of people die each year because of drunk drivers. With impaired judgment, the drunk person is often under the impression that he can handle his alcohol better than he really can.
2. Too much alcohol can cause serious health problems. These problems include, but are not limited to, cirrhosis of the liver, certain cancers, heart disease, and brain damage.
3. A person cannot serve the Lord effectively while intoxicated. Ephesians 5:18 commands believers, "And do not get drunk with wine, for that is debauchery, but be filled with the Spirit." Our bodies are the temples of the Holy Spirit. Intoxicating substances hinder one's ability to obey God through service.

4. Another factor to consider is that, in Bible times, wine was diluted by three parts water to one part wine.[1] This made intoxication very difficult unless one used undiluted "strong drink," which the Bible warned against (Prov. 20:1) except for medicinal purposes (Prov. 31:6).

The Bible has much to say about drug abuse, if one includes alcohol. Drugs such as cocaine, marijuana, LSD, PCP, heroin, methamphetamines, and ecstasy were not known in Bible times, but alcohol was. These substances, including alcohol in excess, are known to impair people's judgment, cause health problems, and hinder their service to the Lord. Some of these substances, such as heroine, cocaine, and methamphetamines, are physically addictive. Withdrawal symptoms can be so severe that hospitalization is required. Other drugs, such as LSD or marijuana, are not physically addictive for most people; however, the social and psychological effects can be devastating.

Another important reason for Christians to abstain from these substances is related to the legal implications. Possession or use of any of these drugs is illegal. Romans 13:1–4 teaches that believers should submit to the ordinances of government. Those who resist these ordinances are resisting God. For people under twenty-one years of age in America, alcohol is also out of the question.

Sometimes objections are raised against the anti-drug-and-alcohol campaign; some point out the health benefits of alcohol in moderation or the medicinal benefits of marijuana. Though there are certain health benefits of alcohol in moderation, the current cultural climate among young people is not a culture of moderation. Furthermore, the fact that it is illegal for those under twenty-one should be kept in mind. College students doing "bong hits" in their dorm room are not doing

---

[1]See Robert H. Stein, "Wine-Drinking in New Testament Times, *Christianity Today,* June 20, 1975, 9-11.

so in order to treat glaucoma or cancer. Laws regarding drugs and alcohol should be respected. Concerning medicinal uses of certain controlled substances, these should be used under the supervision of a physician. Even some prescription drugs can be addictive and debilitating and should be used with caution.

HOW TO GET HELP

The power of the cross is sufficient to help one overcome addictions and other sins. A person must acknowledge his sin and need for help, turn to Christ and ask for forgiveness, and begin to walk a new path. Sometimes walking a new path means saying goodbye to old friends and associations. Because of the physically and psychologically addictive nature of these substances, professional help may be needed. Professional help can come from pastors, counselors, psychologists, and professional agencies devoted to substance abuse. The National Institute on Drug Abuse (NIDA) offers information on the Internet that will better inform you about the nature of substance abuse. Most cities have clinics listed in the phone book where people can go to detoxify. Many churches have a program called "Celebrate Recovery" that incorporates biblical principles into a twelve-step program. You can find a local chapter at www.celebrate recovery.org. Most of these programs focus on adults; however, some churches also have programs for teens. Your local pastor may have other suggestions about how you can get help.

DISCUSSION/APPLICATION:

1. Why do you think so many people in their teens and twenties get involved in drug and alcohol abuse?
2. Suppose you find yourself with a disease that is treatable by a substance that is currently illegal. Should you try to get this substance on the streets? Why or why not?

3. What steps could you take to help a friend who has an obvious problem with substance abuse? Keep in mind that a person usually will not change unless she wants to change.
4. How does the sanctity-of-life principle help form a proper perspective toward substance abuse?

CHRISTIAN LIBERTY

RYAN P. SNUFFER

IN CHAPTER 3, when we were discussing how Christians should regard the Old Testament Law, we said that early Christian leaders established a new idea sometimes referred to as Christian liberty. The purpose of this appendix is to explain in more detail this concept of Christian liberty as it relates to what ethical standards we as Christians should follow.

Throughout church history, the debate between doctrine and cultural traditions has taken many forms. What is accepted as tradition by one generation is sometimes viewed as doctrine by the next. If doctrine is to be understood as clear precepts or ideas from the Bible, then it follows that areas that the Bible does not specifically deal with should not be viewed as Christian doctrine. Christians have not always agreed on what doctrines are essential to the faith; however, the Apostles' Creed summarizes doctrines that almost all believers throughout church history have maintained:

> I believe in God, the Father Almighty, the Creator of
>   heaven and earth,
> And in Jesus Christ, His only Son, our Lord:
> Who was conceived of the Holy Spirit, born of the
>   Virgin Mary,
> Suffered under Pontius Pilate, was crucified, died, and
>   was buried.

He descended into Hell. The third day He arose again
    from the dead.
He ascended into heaven and sits at the right hand of God
    the Father Almighty, whence He shall come to judge
    the living and the dead.
I believe in the Holy Spirit, the holy catholic church,[1]
    the communion of saints, the forgiveness of sins,
    the resurrection of the body, and life everlasting.

Doctrines such as the Apostles' Creed include, but are not necessarily limited to, traditional teachings related to the Trinity, the virgin birth, the inspiration of the Bible, Christ's death on the cross for our sins, and His resurrection.

There are many other teachings of Christianity that are meaningful and important to believers but that are not essential to the faith. Examples of these include the governing structure of a church, denominational names, spiritual gifts, the age of the earth, and the role of women in ministry. Some Christian groups elevate nonessential doctrines to tests of Christian faith. This leads to unnecessary division in the body of Christ. Christians can maintain their beliefs in these nonessential areas and still practice Christian liberty by showing love toward believers who disagree with them in these areas.

Christian liberty can also be thought of in terms of action versus belief. The passages in the New Testament that deal with Christian liberty deal primarily with actions rather than beliefs. Because there is a tendency for some Christians to abuse the idea of liberty, it is important to begin with what Christian liberty is not. Christian liberty is not:

1. *License to sin.* It is never appropriate to sin. Sometimes the Bible does not specifically deal with an issue but there are principles that apply to the issue. For example, though

---

[1]The word "catholic" here is not a reference to the Roman Catholic Church but to the universal church that has existed throughout the ages. The word "catholic" literally means "universal."

the Bible may not specifically condemn heroin use, there are biblical principles that do. A believer's body is the temple of the Holy Spirit. Heroin is a destructive drug that destroys the body. Paul said that he would not be enslaved by anything (1 Cor. 6:12). Heroin is addictive (enslaving). The Bible commands people to submit to the authorities over them. Heroin is illegal. To take heroin is to break the law. These three principles make a strong case that use of heroin, or any other destructive, addictive, illegal substance is wrong.

2. *License to do any action at any time, even if the action itself is not evil.* There are times when something that is not actually wrong should not be done in the presence of people who might be offended by our doing it (Romans 14; 1 Cor. 8:7).

Christian liberty can be summarized by the following ideas:

1. New Testament believers are no longer under the Old Testament Law. The Jerusalem Council in Acts 15 recognized that New Testament believers were no longer under the Law. Paul also deals extensively with this idea in the book of Galatians.

2. Actions and activities not condemned by precept or principle in the New Testament can be enjoyed by believers as long as their conscience does not condemn them and they are not offending those who are weaker in their faith (Rom. 14:1–5, 20–23).

3. There are times when one's liberty must be restrained because the activity would cause a Christian who is weaker in the faith to "stumble" (1 Cor. 8:9–13).

4. Weaker believers can be instructed and helped to grow into stronger believers (Romans 14; 1 Corinthians 8; 10:23–33).

   a. Weaker Christians are those with less understanding about spiritual things (1 Cor. 8:7).

   b. The sin of the weaker Christian is not related to the

action itself, but to his perception of the action (Rom. 14:5; 1 Cor. 10:27–29). It is when a person does something that is inconsistent with his conscience that he sins.

5. All things should be done with a clean conscience and for the glory of God (Rom. 14:22–23; 1 Cor. 10:31).

Christian liberty is an important concept which is dealt with extensively in the New Testament. It has the potential to bring greater unity in the body of Christ. It would do all Christians well to remember that there is only one body of Christ, which has many parts. The diversity within Christ's body helps to complement the diversity that is in the world. Christians are not to be *of the world* in their thinking; however, they must live *in* and try to reach the people of the world with the saving gospel of Christ. This mission can be better realized as Christians assemble themselves around the central teachings of Christianity and learn to gracefully disagree in those areas that are not essential to the faith. Table A.1 illustrates some areas of difference among Christians that are not essential parts of basic Christian doctrine.

Table A.1
Evangelical Traditions and Preferences

Personal appearance	Nonessential doctrines	Worship methodology	Other
Length of hair and facial hair (men), clothing style (women)	Age of the earth, timing of Christ's return, form of church government, role of women in church ministry	Order of service, music styles, the use of creeds, frequency of communion, frequency of church services	Political party, political positions, involvement in social clubs

JESUS' METHOD VS. THE PHARISEES' METHOD

The issue of Christians' relationship to culture is similar to the debate over tradition in Jesus' day. In the Sermon on the Mount,

Jesus pointed out the importance of true inward holiness. He sometimes ignored the established teachings of the Pharisees. The Pharisees had established a complex religious and cultural system, sometimes described as legalism. They began with the Old Testament. They added their interpretation and application of the Law to Jewish culture. One might say that they were attempting to control Jewish culture in the name of religion with legalistic mandates and intimidation techniques. To some degree, they were successful in transforming their culture, but they failed to positively affect the hearts of people.

In Matthew 22, Jesus stated that the two great commands were to love God with all of one's heart, soul, and mind, and to love one's neighbor as oneself. He then said that everything in the Law and the Prophets "depends" on these two commands. In John 13:35 Jesus said that the distinguishing mark of His followers was the love they shared for each other.

Living the "Jesus method" (Table A.2) impacts the believer's testimony to the world. It ensures that one has the right motivation for service to God. It would be impossible for culture not to be impacted if enough Christians lived the Jesus method. People would likely be attracted to the church, and the church would gain more influence. The influence would be indirect rather than direct. The effects would be more profound than any cultural mandates.

Table A.2
The Jesus Method

Love	Result
Love God	Motivation for service is pure
Love God and man	True holiness
Love of the brethren for each other	Positive testimony to the world

In Matthew 23, Jesus blasts the Pharisees for their religious hypocrisy. The Pharisaical method (Table A.3) is detrimental to all those caught within the established system. It confuses, misleads, and offers a false sense of security. Those outside the system are looked down upon and often turned off by religion altogether.

Table A.3
The Pharisaical Method

Legalism	Result
Focus on outward cleanliness	Inwardly unclean (Matt. 23:27)
Imposed standards on others	Students who become cultural clones of their teachers, but are spiritually worse off than their teachers (Matt. 23:15)
Established cultural traditions revered over absolute truth and love	Civil society that is spiritually dead

The Jesus method focuses on people and as a result impacts both people and the culture in which they live. The Pharisaical method focuses on outward conformity to an established culture, and as a result people look good and culture is impacted but there is no genuine spiritual growth. In fact, the Pharisaical method could be worse than having no method, because few people ever see the need to abandon it. Jesus said that the Pharisees were blind men leading the blind.

APPLICATION

Understanding this biblical paradigm should impact preaching and teaching. It should also impact the way in which churches and other Christian institutions are organized. Standards of conduct are important; however, it may be better to have no standards of conduct imposed on people than to have a system that communicates to those within the system that keeping these standards is a true test for holiness. This is not to say that an organization should not have standards. It must. But to call them "Christian" they must have a clear connection with a biblical precept. Such precepts are relatively few in number. Such standards should all stem from the two great commands, since these support the entire moral law. It should also be clearly communicated that outward conformity to these standards will in no way make one holy or right with God.

An example of a standard that relates to the law of love is respect. People should demonstrate respect for God and for each other. A person who has no problem using God's name in vain is not demonstrating proper respect for God. This reflects spiritual immaturity or lack of love for God. A person who would spread false rumors about someone else is not demonstrating respect or love for that person. The same could be said for other clear commands such as adultery, stealing, and disobedience. The way in which problems are dealt with by those in authority should also be guided by love.

A warning must be given at this point. Established traditions are not going to disappear without resistance. Jesus infuriated the Pharisees because He did not respect their traditions. Many today will be just as infuriated when their traditions are not respected. Yet if we take the position that we will not upset the status quo, then we are in danger of misleading new believers. They will continue to believe that they are "okay" with God since they are keeping up with all the traditional standards. Or they will carry around unnecessary guilt resulting from not keeping the established tradition. Worst of all, they will not learn how to love God and their neighbor. To allow people in your sphere of influence to practice the Pharisaical method without accountability is exceedingly unloving.

By the way, it is okay to maintain and even revere age-old traditions. These can be meaningful and positive to a culture; however, they should not be confused with moral absolutes and should never make people feel more spiritual for observing them.

Though Christ did not come to transform culture directly, He did come to change the hearts of men and women who in turn will have an indirect impact on culture as they allow the love of God to be shed abroad in their hearts toward the rest of humanity.

FOR TEACHERS AND SMALL GROUP LEADERS

LOVE YOUR NEIGHBOR is designed as a one-semester course of study for high school or college students. However, for teachers who already teach ethics and have their own notes, books, and audio-visual media on hand, it could easily be adapted to a two-semester course. It is also versatile enough that it could be adapted to small group studies for teens or adults, church youth groups, or college groups.

The text consists of twenty-six chapters with a few practical ideas for assignments or discussion at the end of each chapter. Readers will appreciate the good mix of content and practical application. Chapters are designed so that teachers may move as quickly or as slowly as needed. The material should be rein forced with videos, group activities, and small projects such as those suggested at the end of some of the chapters.

Lesson objectives are provided below for those who choose to use this as a school curriculum. Good lesson objectives are measurable goals for your students to accomplish. You will know your students have met these objectives if they succeed on test day. Feel free to come up with your own objectives as you see fit.

The text is divided into two parts. The first part builds a

biblical and philosophical basis for ethics. The second part covers issues facing young people today. In some chapters, both liberal and conservative perspectives are explained and critiqued. Relevant biblical principles are provided with the various issues.

One of the goals of all sincere Bible teachers should be the spiritual maturity of their students' thought lives. Though this goal is not easily measured, teachers should include relevant passages of Scripture in each lesson to help direct them toward this goal. Only the Holy Spirit can produce faith in God and Christ. Teachers can choose whether or not to quiz on the reading of the Bible passages.

The primary purpose of this text is to encourage people to think critically from a Christian perspective about the moral issues they face. The content is well-reasoned and accurate, though at times abbreviated. Readers should understand that their primary goal in this course is to be introduced to Christian ethics, not to master the subject.

INTRODUCTORY QUESTIONS

Whether in an academic setting or in a home or church group, it is important to get people interested in the topics before they are covered. The following questions correspond with the chapters in the book. They are designed to provoke critical thinking about the particular subjects, with the hope of creating greater interest in the subjects before reading about them. These questions can make great discussion starters for small groups or classes of students:

1. *The Nature of God.* Can God make a rock so big that He cannot pick it up? How can the finite grasp anything about the infinite?
2. *The Nature of Morality.* Did God choose what would be right and wrong for humans, or are these things part of who He is?

3. *The Old Testament Law.* Why do Christians acknowledge only certain parts of the Old Testament as applicable to them? Isn't it wrong to pick and choose certain parts of the Bible and avoid others? Isn't all of the Bible equally important?

4. *The Heart of the Law.* What is the most important command given in the entire Bible?

5. *Relativistic Ethical Systems.* Does morality (right and wrong) change from time to time and from culture to culture?

6. *Absolutist Ethical Systems (Part 1).* Isn't it arrogant for anyone to think that his way is the only way when it comes to morality?

7. *Absolutist Ethical Systems (Part 2).* How can we communicate to people a system of absolute morality without coming across as arrogant?

8. *Facing the Issues.* There are so many ethical issues out there that people are supposed to keep up with. Before jumping into the particular issues, consider how the principle of love can broadly apply to different moral dilemmas and scenarios.

   How would you describe the color of a red rose to someone who is red-green colorblind? Before beginning this chapter, get together in groups of three or four and come up with a plan of how you would describe the rose. Compare your plan with the plans of other groups. What are the best ideas? Why is this so difficult?

9. *Lying.* Is it ever loving to lie to someone? Think of examples of how lying as such is unloving.

10. *Cheating.* Who is the real victim when a person cheats?

11. *Stealing.* Would you ever steal in order to provide food for someone you love?

12. *Civil Disobedience.* Should a person have to ask God for forgiveness every time he or she breaks a human law? In other words, is it ever morally permissible to break a human law?

13. *Economic Inequality.* Do you think that Jesus implied that you should help poor strangers when He said to love your neighbor?

With so much poverty in the world, no single person or church can help everyone. What impoverished group should the church see as a priority: The homeless in its town? Working families in areas that cannot afford a reasonable standard of living? The poor in other countries? Or some other group?

14. *Homosexuality.* Why is the issue of homosexuality becoming so mainstream in politics, churches, and the media (though in years past people hardly spoke of it in public)?

15. *Heterosexual Sin.* How much control can we have over our sexual desires when we are bombarded with sexual images from so many directions?

16. *Pornography.* Suppose a person had a choice between receiving a check today for $50,000 or one check a week for a year (fifty-two weeks) for $5,000 each. Which would you choose? Most intelligent people would choose the latter, which would result in receiving $260,000. This is because most people understand simple math, or they understand the principle of delayed gratification in order to gain more. Why is it, then, that in the area of sexuality, people are willing to give up something better in the future in order to gain a smaller amount of satisfaction now?

17. *Marriage and Divorce.* Why do you think that divorce is sometimes harder on the children than on the divorcing husband and wife?

18. *Ecological Issues.* How can we apply the "love your neighbor" principle to the subject of taking care of the planet?

19. *Ethics and Politics.* Should moral issues be kept out of the political arena? Why or why not?

20. *Abortion.* How would you feel if your daughter became pregnant while in high school? How would you feel if she had an abortion without your permission?

21. *Euthanasia.* Do you think that a person has a basic human right to be able to die with dignity (quickly and

painlessly rather than suffering in a hospital bed hooked up to machines for an extended time)?

22. *Cloning.* Imagine a world in which human clones lived among us. How would you feel about a girlfriend/boyfriend or spouse if you found out he or she was a clone and that the "original person" was still living somewhere?

23. *Stem Cell Research and Other Biomedical Issues.* Is it loving or unloving to destroy human embryos in order to help living humans with debilitating diseases?

24. *Capital Punishment.* How should the "love your neighbor" principle apply to the criminal?

25. *War.* How should the "love your neighbor" principle apply to civilians living in a country with which your country is at war?

26. *Substance Abuse.* If a person is hurting only her own body when using drugs, then how does the "love your neighbor" principle apply to the issue of drug abuse?

COURSE OBJECTIVES

1. The students will be able to outline the philosophical basis for the idea of absolute moral truth claims.

2. The students will be able to compare and contrast the relativistic and absolutist approaches to ethics.

3. The students will be able to refute weak moral approaches to specific ethical issues.

4. The students will be able to apply their knowledge of ethical issues to real-life decisions they will face.

5. The students will read, memorize, and apply Scriptures that relate to various points in the text.

6. The students will sharpen their critical thinking skills regarding decisions they will face.

LESSON OBJECTIVES

These lesson objectives correspond with the twenty-six chapters in the book:

1. To define attributes of the theistic God.

To distinguish between God's infinite and personal attributes.

2. To define morality from an absolute truth perspective.

3. To distinguish among the three aspects of the Old Testament Law.

4. To define the proper motive for holy living.

5. To define relativistic ethical approaches.

   To critique relativistic ethical approaches.

6. To define absolutist ethical systems.

   To critique absolutist ethical systems.

7. To define absolutist ethical systems.

   To critique absolutist ethical systems.

8. To contrast aspects of secular humanism with theism.

   To define the sanctity-of-life and sovereignty-of-God principles.

9. To define a "lie" from a biblical perspective.

   To apply the concept of lying to the various ethical approaches.

10. To refute the typical reasons for cheating with practical and spiritual considerations.

11. To list examples of various types of stealing.

    To identify reasons why stealing is wrong.

12. To define various approaches to civil disobedience.

    To defend biblical submissionism as the proper approach regarding civil disobedience.

13. To list biblical reasons to help the poor.

    To answer objections to helping the poor.

14. To list pro-gay positions.

    To respond to pro-gay positions.

    To list biblical principles regarding the gay lifestyle.

15. To list the purposes of sex.

    To consider the dangers of sex outside of marriage.

16. To memorize Romans 12:1–2.

    To formulate a plan to protect yourself from sexual immorality.

17. To interpret key Bible passages about divorce.

18. To list biblical principles related to ecology.

    To analyze ecological issues in light of Scripture.

19. To prove that all societies legislate morality.

20. To define various views on abortion.

    To refute pro-choice arguments.

21. To define terms and categories related to euthanasia.

    To apply biblical principles in formulating an acceptable approach to euthanasia.

22. To define cloning.

    To distinguish between cloning to produce humans and cloning for medical research.

    To critique the idea of human cloning.

23. To define various biomedical issues and outline their ethical implications.

24. To define terms related to capital punishment.

    To refute reconstructionism as a viable option for Christians today.

25. To define three ethical views on war.

    To defend selectivism as the best ethical approach to war.

26. To define substance abuse.

    To identify ways those involved in substance abuse can get help.

MORE HELP FOR TEACHERS

The study of Christian ethics cannot be exhausted in just one semester. This book is not meant to replace individual study and training on the part of the teacher. Throughout the book, footnotes are provided so that teachers can readily access more in-depth information from other sources. The more familiar you are with this material, the better you will be able to communicate it to your students, and the better they will be prepared to communicate it to others. Following is a list of books and other resources to help teachers better prepare themselves to teach such a course:

Copan, Paul. *True for You, but Not for Me*. Minneapolis: Bethany, 1998.

The Critical Thinking Community. www.criticalthinking.org.

Focus on the Family. www.family.org.

Geisler, Norman. *Christian Ethics: Options and Issues.* Grand Rapids, Mich.: Baker, 1989.

Geisler, Norman, and Josh McDowell. *Love Is Always Right: A Defense of the One Moral Absolute.* Nashville: Word, 1996.

Lewis, C. S. *The Abolition of Man.* San Francisco: Harper Collins, 2001. First published in 1944.

Lewis, C. S. *Mere Christianity.* San Francisco: HarperCollins, 2001. First published in 1952.

McDowell, Josh. *Beyond Belief to Convictions.* Wheaton, Ill.: Tyndale, 2002.

GRADING

- Give frequent quizzes and tests to ensure that students are learning the content of the text. Include vocabulary terms, Scripture memory, and short-answer questions in which students are asked to refute or defend a particular viewpoint.
- Have students keep the notes and assignments in a notebook. Collect the notebooks from time to time to evaluate student participation and effort.
- Have students keep a journal throughout the semester. Most chapters will provide a suggested reading from the Bible that relates to the chapter. Have students meditate on the passage and record their thoughts in a journal. Monitor their participation.
- Use the discussion/application sections for ideas for assignments to grade.
- Set aside a couple of weeks at the end of the course for in-class debates. Students will need to be given instructions at least a month in advance. Students can do a three-to-five-page research paper on their topic as support material for their debate. The research paper could count as one or two test grades.

Teachers should supplement the material with newspaper articles, videos, and other resources. There is a recommended reading list at the end of many of the chapters for those students who are highly motivated. This will not only make the subject more interesting; it will also help the students apply these ideas to their lives as they see how these concepts relate to the world in which they live. It is important that teachers help students to move from the theoretical to the practical. Some high school and college students will not do this without guidance.

This text is only a brief introduction to each of the topics addressed. Few will master the subject. Not all ethical dilemmas are easily solved. However, readers should enjoy and benefit from this fresh and practical approach to Christian ethics. It is our prayer that every reader will have a stronger faith and greater discernment by the time he or she reaches the end of the book.

RECOMMENDED SCHEDULE FOR ONE-SEMESTER COURSE

Unit 1: Introduction to Christian Ethics

Week 1: Orientation, Introduction, and the Nature of God (Lesson 1)
Week 2: The Nature of Morality (Lesson 2)
Week 3: The Old Testament Law, The Heart of the Law (Lessons 3–4)
Week 4: Relativistic Ethical Systems, Absolutist Ethical Systems Part 1 (Lessons 5–6)
Week 5: Absolutist Ethical Systems Part 2, Facing the Issues (Lessons 7–8)

Unit 2: The Issues

Week 6: Lying, Cheating (Chapters 9–10)
Week 7: Stealing, Civil Disobedience (Chapters 11–12)
Week 8: Economic Injustice, Homosexuality (Chapters 13–14)
Week 9: Heterosexual Sin, Pornography (Chapters 15–16)
Week 10: Marriage and Divorce (Chapters 17)
Week 11: Ecological Issues (Chapters 18)
Week 12: Ethics and Politics, Abortion (Chapters 19–20)
Week 13: Euthanasia, Cloning (Chapters 21–22)
Week 14: Stem Cell Research and Other Biomedical Issues (Chapter 23)
Week 15: Capital Punishment (Chapter 24)
Week 16: War, Substance Abuse (Chapters 25–26)
Weeks 17 and 18: Appendix A, Debates, Review, Catch-up, Exams

GLOSSARY

absolute truth. Something that is true for all people at all times and in all situations; the view that regards truth as fixed or unchanging. See also **truth**.

antinomianism. An approach to ethics that refuses to acknowledge any authority or claim to absolute moral truth; lawlessness.

apologetics. A rational defense of the Christian faith; a reasoned defense of a Christian's worldview or religious convictions.

atheism. A worldview that denies the existence of God.

conflicting absolutism. An approach to ethics that recognizes many absolutes that sometimes conflict with each other, in which case one is obligated to choose the lesser of two evils.

deity. Either a false god or the true God; something that is worshiped as divine.

ethics. The study of standards of right and wrong behavior.

finite. Having boundaries or limitations; being limited in existence.

generalism. An approach to ethics that acknowledges general rules and guidelines but no absolutes; general norms are determined by the majority in a society.

graded absolutism. An approach to ethics that recognizes many absolutes that sometimes conflict with each other, in which case one is obligated to choose the greater good.

infinite. Without boundaries or limitations.

inspiration. Related to theology, the act of God working through prophets and apostles as they wrote Scripture to ensure that they were affirming only what is true.

law of noncontradiction. In logic, a law that states that opposite ideas cannot both be true at the same time or in the same sense; the opposite of what is true is false.

moral absolutism. The view that what is right or wrong can be applied to every culture and time and person.

moral relativism. The belief that regards truth as having no objective basis and says that what can be considered right or wrong can vary from time to time, culture to culture, and person to person.

pantheism. A worldview that says all is God and God is all; God is the universe.

philosophy. The study of human thought about the meaning of life or ethics.

rational. Able to reason or think clearly; reasonable or sensible.

sanctity-of-life principle. The concept that human life has value because God created it and it bears His image.

situationism. An approach to ethics that recognizes the one moral absolute of love. All ethical dilemmas can be decided by determining what the most loving action would be in a given situation.

sovereignty-of-God principle. The concept that God rules over the universe; in ethics, the recognition that God has the right to rule over life-and-death matters.

theism. Worldview that acknowledges a personal, infinite God who created the universe.

tolerance. Willingness to allow others to have and to express their beliefs and live their lives as they choose within the law, even while disagreeing with their beliefs and life choices.

truth. That which corresponds to the facts; "telling it like it is."

worldview. The way in which a person perceives the world, especially related to a philosophical or religious perspective.

GENERAL INDEX

SCRIPTURE INDEX